P9-BZL-827

Hiking Virginia's National Forests

Hiking Virginia's National Forests

Fourth Edition

by

Karin Wuertz-Schaefer

An East Woods Book

The Globe Pequot Press

Chester, Connecticut

Copyright © 1977, 1980, 1983, 1989 by The Globe Pequot Press

The Globe Pequot Press assumes no liabilty for accidents happening to, or injuries sustained by, readers who engage in the activities described in this book.

All rights reserved. No part of this book may be reproduced or transmitted in any form by any means, electronic or mechanical, including photocopying and recording, or by any information storage and retrieval system except as may be expressly permitted by the 1976 Copyright Act or by the publisher. Requests for permission should be made in writing to The Globe Pequot Press, 138 West Main Street, Chester, Connecticut 06412.

Maps created by Robert J. Schaefer

Library of Congress Cataloging-in-Publication Data

Wuertz-Schaarfer, Karin
        Hiking Virginia's National Forests / by Karin Wuerts-Schaefer – 4th ed.

        p. cm.
    "An East Woods book."
    Bibliography: p. 182
    ISBN 0-87106-526-6
    1. Hiking–George Washington National Forest
 (Va. and W. Va.) – Guide-books. 3. George Washington
 4. Jefferson National Forest – Guide-books.
    I. Title.
GV199.42.G45W84 1989
917.55 – dc20

                                                    89–32602
                                                         CIP

Manfactured in the United States of America
Fourth Edition/Second Printing

This book is the result of the combined efforts of local members of the Sierra Club and the Virginia Wilderness Committee, who invite all who enjoy and cherish the beautiful Virginia mountains to join in their efforts to protect them.

Sierra Club
730 Polk Street
San Francisco, CA 94109

Virginia Wilderness Committtee
Route 1, Box 156
Swoope, VA 24479

Acknowledgments

I would like to thank the many people without whom this book would never have come into being. My gratitude goes to all the scouts who did most of the leg work: John Appelquist, Jan Beyers, Tammy Browning, Ernie Dickerman, Harvey Ferris, Marc Frazer, Sam Gage, David Jenkins, Michael Maguire, Eddie Nance, Dan Reichel, Bob Simms, Jon and Sally Soest, Matt Vester, and the members of the William and Mary Biology Club. The staff of both national forests also has been very helpful.

Constance Stallings deserves thanks for her support and suggestions throughout the project. Lee Bowen and Jim Murray were ready with their help in a pinch.

And last, but not least, I am grateful to my husband, Bob, who first suggested the book and who has patiently suffered through it all. His help in scouting, taking trail notes, reading the manuscript, drawing the maps, and doing countless other chores was invaluable. Without it the project would have foundered long ago.

Contents

Introduction 15
Finding Your Way in the Woods 21
Climate, Terrain, and Equipment 25
Outdoor Ethics 29

GEORGE WASHINGTON NATIONAL FOREST

1. BIG SCHLOSS AREA 34
Mill Mountain Trail................................. 39
Halfmoon Trail....................................... 40
Big Blue Trail 42
Peer Trail 45
Mill Creek Trail...................................... 47
Little Stony Creek Trail 48
Little Sluice Mountain Trail 50
Bread Road Trail 52
Cedar Creek Trail 53
Cut-off Trail... 54

2. LAUREL FORK AREA 57
Laurel Fork Trail..................................... 62
Buck Run Trail 64
Locust Spring Trail.................................. 66
Slabcamp Run Trail................................. 67
Bearwallow Run Trail 68
Middle Mountain Trail 69
Christian Run Trail 71

3. RAMSEY'S DRAFT WILDERNESS 73
Shenandoah Mountain Trail 77
Ramsey's Draft Trail................................ 80
Hardscrabble Knob Trail 83
Jerry's Run Trail..................................... 84
Wild Oak Trail.. 85

Tearjacket Trail 87
Bald Ridge Trail 88
Sinclair Hollow Trail 90

4. CRAWFORD MOUNTAIN AREA 93
Crawford Knob Trail 97
Crawford Mountain Trail 98
Chimney Hollow Trail 100

5. ELLIOTT KNOB AREA 101
Elliott Knob Road 104
Falls Hollow Trail 106
North Mountain Trail 107
Cold Spring Trail 110

JEFFERSON NATIONAL FOREST

6. JAMES RIVER FACE WILDERNESS 114
Appalachian Trail 118
Piney Ridge Trail 120
Belfast Trail 121
Gunter Ridge Trail 123
Balcony Falls Trail 125
Sulphur Spring Trail 126

7. MOUNTAIN LAKE WILDERNESS 129
Biological-Station-to-Bear-Cliff Trail 134
Bear-Cliff-to-Bald-Knob Trail 135
Chestnut Trail/War Spur Overlook/War Spur
    Connector to Appalachian Trail 136
Mann's Bog 137
Appalachian Trail 138
Potts Mountain Trail 140
White Rocks Trail 142
John's Creek Trail 143
George's Cut Hollow and Harvey Hollow Trails 145

8. PETERS MOUNTAIN WILDERNESS 147

Dickinson Gap Trail...150
Appalachian Trail (southwest section)..................................151
Appalachian Trail (northeast section) 153
Dismal Branch Trail..155
Kelly Flats Trail..156
North Fork Trail..157
Dixon Branch Trail 158

9. MILL CREEK AREA 161
Appalachian Trail..164
Mill Creek Trail 166

10. MOUNT ROGERS NATIONAL RECREATION
     AREA...169
Mount Rogers Trail...173
Appalachian Trail..174
Summit Trail 177
Wilburn Ridge Trail 178
Pine Mountain Trail 179
Lewis Fork Trail 180

Suggested Readings 182

Photo Credits

Page 2: Big Schloss Area by Karin Wuertz-Schaefer.
Page 14: Mount Rogers National Recreation Area by Eddie Nance.
Page 20: Ramsey's Draft Wilderness by Kathleen Borland.
Page 24: Elliot Knob Area by Bob Simms.
Page 32: Big Schloss Area by Karin Wuertz-Schaefer.
Page 56: Laurel Fork Area by Robert J. Schaefer.
Page 92: Crawford Mountain Area by Robert J. Schaefer.
Page 112: James River Face Wilderness by John Applequist.
Page 128: Mountain Lake Wilderness by John Applequist.
Page 160: Big Schloss Area by Karin Wuertz-Schaefer.
Page 168: Mount Rogers National Recreation Area by Eddie Nance.

List of Maps

Page 12: George Washington and Jefferson national forests
Page 36: Big Schloss
Page 58: Laurel Fork
Page 74: Ramsey's Draft
Page 94: Crawford Mountain
Page 102: Elliot Knob
Page 116: James River Face
Page 130: Mountain Lake
Page 148: Peters Mountain
Page 162: Mill Creek
Page 170: Mount Rogers

Hiking Virginia's National Forests

GEORGE WASHINGTON NATIONAL FOREST

1 BIG SCHLOSS
2 LAUREL FORK
3 RAMSEY'S DRAFT
4 CRAWFORD MOUNTAIN
5 ELLIOTT KNOB

JEFFERSON NATIONAL FOREST

6 JAMES RIVER FACE
7 MOUNTAIN LAKE
8 PETERS MOUNTAIN
9 MILL CREEK
10 MOUNT ROGERS

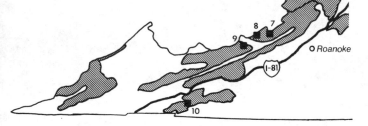

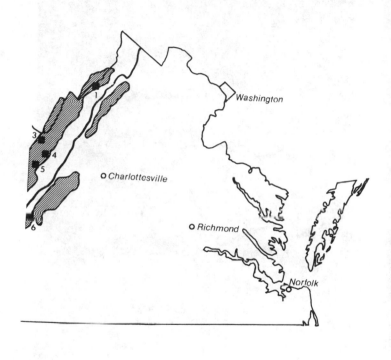

Introduction

The national forests of Virginia—George Washington National Forest in the northwest and Jefferson National Forest in the southwest—encompass large areas of mountains and forests laced with clear streams. Wildlife is abundant, and many trails crisscross the region.

Looking at road maps for most regions of the United States, you will see large patches of green, indicating national forests. This is misleading, for although national forest boundaries have been authorized by Congress, there is much privately owned land within them. The U.S. Forest Service has not been able to purchase all of the land in the authorized regions. In the past, logged-over tracts were often offered for sale to the federal government because the owners had no further use for them and did not want to invest money in reforestation programs. But now many of these regions are beginning to mature and assume appearances close to their original ones.

Trying to compile a trail guide to all of both national forests in Virginia would have been a monumental task. Instead, we have selected ten areas—five in each forest—that are outstanding for various reasons. These tracts are largely self-contained units bounded by roads and often by private land. Human intrusion is minimal, and each area, in its own way, is unique.

We want this book to give you a taste for hiking in the forests. There are many additional places that have good trails and are worth exploring. A number of wilderness areas in Virginia have been established by Congress since this book was first published in 1977. Many recreation sites and campgrounds (generally levying a small fee) exist. But wilderness camping is often available by hiking a few miles along a trail.

Even in the places covered by this book, you may find obscure and unmaintained trails. We have tried to describe all the ones that can be found and followed with reasonable care, but surprises are still possible. The Forest Service budget provides some money for trail maintenance, and their crews do most of the heavy work such as cleaning severe obstructions from the trails. Citizens' organizations, relying on volunteers, can maintain only a few trails.

The Appalachian Trail (AT) is part of the trail system in many areas covered by this guide. If you are interested in learning more about the AT—especially elsewhere in the state—we suggest you obtain a copy of *Guide to the Appalachian Trail in Central and Southwestern Virginia*, published by the Appalachian Trail Conference in Harpers Ferry, WV 25425.

In some places you will find small cabins owned and maintained by the Potomac Appalachian Trail Club. These cabins are locked, but the general public as well as club members may make reservations for their use. Contact the club for additional information well in advance of your trip. The address: Potomac Appalachian Trail Club, 1718 N Street, N.W., Washington, D.C. 20036; telephone (202) 638-5306.

Much of the George Washington and Jefferson national forests is habitat for the black bear and the bobcat, although both are extremely wary and rarely seen. On our hikes and camping trips we have seen and heard skunks, opposums, and raccoons as well as beavers, squirrels, and other rodents.

Bird life is varied—turkeys, ruffed grouse, ravens, pileated woodpeckers, and whippoorwills are just a few of the many, many species, both summer and winter residents, that we have identified. You may find additional denizens of the woods too numerous to list. A good number of streams support trout. Please remember that the hunting and fishing laws of the state of Virginia are applicable in those portions of the national forests that lie within the state's boundaries. Some trails also cross into West Virginia, and, of course, West Virginia hunting and fishing laws apply there. We have not attempted to define political boundaries in this book. If in doubt, check with the District Ranger's office.

National forests differ from national parks in several respects. The national forests are administered by the Forest Service under the U.S. Department of Agriculture, while national parks are managed by the National Park Service under the U.S. Department of the Interior. The management philosophy for these public resources is also profoundly different. National forests are managed under the multiple-use concept and are open to many kinds of human activity, including logging, road building, dams, hunting, fishing, hiking, and camping. Not so in the national parks. They are closed to logging and hunting, and they are largely protected from dams, highways, and other such encroachments.

In areas that are part of the National Wilderness Preservation System, whether located in national forests or national parks, the land is protected in its pristine condition. Within definite boundaries set by law, all impact of human activity is kept to a minimum, and no permanent human structures, such as roads, dams, or buildings, are allowed. Logging and the use of motorized vehicles are against the law. Pursuits that do not scar the land are permitted and in fact invited: hiking and backpacking, camping, fishing, cross-country skiing, hunting (except in national parks), and more. Here you will find peace and solitude and quiet and relief from the hustle and bustle of everyday life.

One unusual aspect of this book must be mentioned: All distances and area measurements are given in the metric system with the U.S. measures in parentheses. The same is true of temperature: The first figure is in degrees Celsius and the second in degrees Fahrenheit. Thus you should have no difficulty in relating the new metric values to those of your previous experience. The only exception to the above is that a few short distances are given only in meters, with no equivalent in yards. Because one yard is only slightly less than one meter, we would have been repeating the same figure in most cases.

The contour elevations shown on the maps are expressed in feet to simplify comparison with U.S. Geological Survey (USGS) maps. The contour interval is 250 feet (76 meters).

All distances given in the individual trail descriptions are approximate and should not be taken as the final word. Many trails twist and turn too much for anyone to keep track of them with absolute accuracy, and the convolutions cannot be measured from maps because they do not show up well.

Numbered Forest Development roads, which generally are well-maintained gravel roads, are abbreviated "FDR" throughout the text.

A word of caution: Do not depend totally on trail signs mentioned in this book. The signs are subject to vandalism by both bears and humans and may have disappeared by the time you get there. Most of the trailheads, though, can still be found because the signposts usually remain standing. You can help by notifying Forest Service personnel about missing trail signs.

There is talk in Forest Service circles about replacing trail names on signs with numbers, in the hope of reducing the incidence of people taking them home as souvenirs. We have attempted to include as many of the numbers as possible.

Finding Your Way in the Woods

When you are hiking in the woods, some method of orientation is necessary. Trail maps are provided for each area covered in this book. Nevertheless, you may want additional information on access roads, private inholdings, or topography.

The U.S. Forest Service issues maps for both George Washington and Jefferson national forests and more detailed maps for many ranger districts within them. These maps carry much useful information on campgrounds and trails. They are also good to have if you are planning to investigate some areas not listed in this guide.

For copies of these maps, write to:
Supervisor
George Washington National Forest
Harrison Plaza
101 N. Main Street, P.O. Box 233
Harrisonburg, VA 22801

Supervisor
Jefferson National Forest
210 Franklin Road, S.W.
Roanoke, VA 24011

For detailed topographic information, the U.S. Geological Survey maps, on a scale of 1:24000, are available for all areas in the national forests. In addition, the Forest Service now reprints the U.S. Geological Survey maps overlaid with land ownership information. These maps, issued as quadrangles, generally follow latitudes and longitudes, which are conveniently established reference lines. Unfortunately, however, area boundaries rarely coincide with these invented divisions, so you may need two or more adjacent maps to cover the region of your hikes. We have listed all the quadrangles you will need under each area covered in this book.

You can obtain quadrangles from the U.S. Geological Survey, 1200 S. Eads Street, Arlington, VA 22202. And while you are writing, ask also for an index map of Virginia, which will give you the names of all quadrangles in the state. For Forest Service maps, contact the appropriate forest supervisor's office. The charge is $2.50 per map. Sometimes large-scale maps are available for wilderness areas in the forests.

Contour maps are easy to read once you have mastered the skill. A mountaintop usually appears as a small circle, with the very top marked by a symbol and a figure giving the elevation. Larger contour lines delineate the rest of the mountain, joining all points of equal elevation. The closer the contour lines are to each other, the steeper the hillside. Check the margin of each map for the exact interval between contours, as it may vary from map to map.

On USGS maps, contour lines appear in brown, constructed features are indicated in black or red, streams and water are blue, wooded areas are shaded in green, and clearings are white. Some trails shown may have disappeared since the maps were published, so you may have to retrace your steps or do some bushwhacking.

If you go cross-country—even in areas listed in this guide—carry a map and compass. Good inexpensive compasses, usually with operating instructions, are available at outdoor stores. Make sure you know how to use both map and compass before you leave on your trip.

When hiking or bushwhacking, always pay attention to the lay of the land—a stream on the right, a steep hillside on the left, later a clearing on the left and a valley on the right, and so on. This will help you to determine your position on the map and the distance you have covered or have left to hike, as well as to orient yourself in the right direction.

The areas described in this book are hardly big enough to get seriously lost in, but a compass might prove useful nonetheless. If you do not have one and you do get lost, a good rule is to head downhill. Most mountain valleys have a stream; find one and follow it downward. Chances are you will strike a road after some miles.

If you run into serious trouble while hiking, such as an injury to a member of the party, remember that the magic number is three. Blow three times in a row on a whistle; in an open area, spread three ponchos, three shirts, or build three small, smoky fires. Three of anything is the accepted distress call. If your party is large enough, send two or more people for help. But at least one member of the group should stay with the injured person and keep him or her warm while you wait for help to arrive.

Climate, Terrain, and Equipment

The highest point in the George Washington National Forest is Elliott Knob at 1,361 meters (4,463 feet) and in the Jefferson National Forest, Mount Rogers at 1,747 meters (5,729 feet). Mount Rogers is also the highest point in Virginia.

The terrain of Virginia's mountains is varied. Some trails afford easy afternoon hikes; others are steep and rugged. A person in moderately good physical condition should have little trouble negotiating most of these trails. Our trail descriptions will tell you about the exact terrain covered, including the difference in elevation to be negotiated on each trail.

Most regions described in this book lend themselves equally well to day hikes and to weekend backpacking trips. They are relatively small and can be hiked through easily in one day, especially if you have a car shuttle at the other end for one-way hikes. We have also enjoyed packing in a few miles, picking a good campsite, and exploring the surroundings from this base camp.

There are shelters in some areas, especially along the Appalachian Trail, but be prepared to find them already occupied. The AT is one of the most popular trails around. There are also a number of U.S. Forest Service campgrounds scattered throughout the national forests. Some are free; others levy a small fee.

A tent, tarp, or other shelter for the night is good to have along to keep you dry in case the weather turns bad and to protect you from the frequently heavy dew.

If you plan to camp out, select a tent or sleeping site on a higher spot than the surrounding area, even if it is ever so slight. Otherwise you may wake up—as we once did—in a puddle of water. Make sure you get to your campsite while there is plenty of daylight left, because the high ground can be hard to spot.

Afternoon showers in the summer are common, particularly at high elevations. It is advisable to carry a poncho or rain jacket on even the brightest summer days, and especially if you plan to stay out overnight. A rain jacket can also serve nicely as a windbreaker on an exposed mountaintop or rock outcrop, where you should have something extra to wear when you sit down for lunch after a long, hot hike.

In the winter you will encounter other hazards. Make sure you have *plenty* of warm clothes along. On an exposed peak, the windchill factor can get down to dangerous levels. Besides carrying enough clothes to keep you warm, be sure to take lots of food and water. Only through this combination can you expect to maintain your body temperature comfortably.

Hypothermia is a lowering of the core temperature of the body that can be brought on by a lack of any of the above essentials. It can lead to death within two hours. Violent shivering, difficulty in speaking, blue and puffy skin, and erratic movements are hypothermia's warning signs. If you have any of these symptoms, get under shelter immediately. Take off wet clothes and put on more, dry ones—preferably of wool or one of the modern synthetic materials such as polypropylene. Get into your sleeping bag. Drink lots of hot, sweet things, such as coffee or tea with sugar or chocolate.

By the way, alcohol is quite the wrong thing to drink. Rather than help, it will aggravate the situation.

Sunburn is possible, especially if there is snow on the ground reflecting the sun's rays. Don't forget your sunglasses, for snow blindness is quite painful.

On the trail, wear a pair of sturdy, comfortable shoes with good traction on the soles. Boots will provide some measure of protection against turned ankles. If you plan to hike a trail with many stream crossings, you may prefer wearing sneakers, especially if the trail itself is level.

Long treatises have been written on sleeping bags, and there is little we can add. But in the mountains even summer nights can get chilly. Take a bag that is warmer than you think you will need. It's easy to stick an arm or foot out of the bag at night if you get too hot, but it is difficult to compensate for too cold a bag. And you should keep in mind your personal disposition and make allowances for that. If you are a "reptile" and are always cold, as I am, add a few degrees to the low-comfort limit of the sleeping bag supplied by the manufacturer and you should be okay in weather down to the adjusted temperature.

In summer, be sure to take along some kind of headgear—if not a hat, a scarf or bandana—especially if you are subject to headaches during exposure to bright sun. Although most of the trails described in this book are heavily forested, several are quite open, and there you may need protection. Unfortunately, as the gypsy moth spreads southward, you can expect to find hot sun under the denuded branches of the forest where you had hoped for cool shade.

The Forest Service does not test water regularly and thus cannot identify safe drinking water sources. During most of the year, you can find water in springs or streams at many points along the trails. We do not recommend drinking from streams. We suggest you carry water from a known, safe source. For longer camping trips, where carrying water is not feasible, either bring a water purification kit, chlorine tablets, or boil your water for five minutes. The last option, done in the evening and left standing overnight—covered, of course—should provide cool water for your canteen and the next day's hike.

Hunting is subject to state regulation on all national forest lands. The woods are often overrun with hunters during the deer season. If you can, avoid hiking and camping or backpacking then. If you choose to go anyway, do wear some blaze orange and avoid wearing clothing or packs with white or any light color on them. If in doubt, check with the district ranger's office for advice.

Outdoor Ethics

The most important rule in the out-of-doors is, "If you carry it in full, you can carry it out empty." That applies to all things you use on a hiking or camping/backpacking trip.

Empty cans should be flattened or crushed. Remove the bottom and step on them. Flat, they and the lids will occupy practically no space in your pack. If you take soda or beer cans, stomp on them when empty and they will become considerably less bulky. Burying cans is unacceptable because small animals might dig them up and it would take too long for the cans to decompose. A paper or plastic bag comes in handy. Accumulate all your trash in it, and you will have only one item to dispose of when you meet a trash can back in civilization.

The same pack-out principle, of course, applies to all glass, plastic, and to almost every other item invented by humans. And if you want to be better than some of the people who traveled the trail before you, pick up some of the junk they left behind and carry it out, thus leaving the area a bit cleaner than you found it.

If you have a campfire, burn all paper, candy wrappers, and similar things you want to dispose of. Watch out for aluminum foil, though. It won't burn and will have to be packed out with the cans.

Try to keep your campfire small. A large fire consumes a lot of wood, and a big stone ring is unsightly. Remember, too, never to cut living wood for your fire. Usually there is enough dead wood lying about for everybody. And if there is' not, so much more the need to burn what little there is sparingly in a small fire. Do not build fires on warm, dry, and/or windy days. Both Virginia and West Virginia have a fire season in the summer when no open fires are allowed in the woods. Again, check with the district ranger's office for dates and advice.

Using a butane or gasoline stove will also help to conserve wood. In addition, your food will cook faster because the heat concentration under the pot will be greater. It will also save you some work, for wood fires produce awfully sooty pots.

If you do light a fire, douse it well before you leave, then stir the ashes down to the very bottom. Wait a few minutes and stir again. Feel the ashes with your bare hand to make sure they are cold. If hot embers are left on the bottom of the pit, they can slowly burn down to organic matter underneath and start a wildfire.

Try to obliterate all traces of your stay, including the fire ring. Put the stones back where you found them, turning the black side under. Scatter the wet ashes, and cover up the scorched area with pebbles or leaves if there are any in the immediate vicinity.

When looking for a campsite, you may find the campsites of previous visitors, often recognizable by fire rings. Use one of these established campsites rather than setting up yet another a short distance away.

If you are leading a group, keep the size down to a manageable number. More than fifteen people usually become a chore. Try to match up participants to make full use of the tents carried. Taking fewer tents will occupy a minimum of camping space and therefore disturb the environment the least, not to mention the lighter loads on your backs.

Avoid congested campsites, whether you are alone or in a group. If your group is large, plan on having alternative campsites available. You should be able to set up two or even three tents away from the crowd.

Dispose of soapy and dirty used water well away from streams. Dumping it into creeks is unacceptable. In addition to polluting the source of supply, it could be harmful to fellow campers downstream who use the creeks for cooking and drinking.

A word on sanitation: Bury all your wastes. Pick a site well away from any open water—at least 15 meters (50 feet)—and dig a small hole 20 to 25 centimeters (8 to 10 inches) in diameter and no more than 15 to 20 centimeters (6 to 8 inches) deep. Keep the sod intact if possible. After use, fill the hole with the soil and tramp in the sod. Nature will do the rest in a few days. Carrying a small digging tool like a garden trowel is a good idea.

Follow the same procedure for leftover food that you want to dispose of. Black bears do live in the mountains of Virginia and, although they are shy and normally avoid humans, it is better not to tempt them to come close to a campsite with the smell of unburied food.

Should you decide on a visit to our national forests around the Fourth of July, please remember that this is *not* the place for fireworks. While perhaps appropriate at home or maybe in a city park, the national forests (and national parks) were set aside for peace, quiet, and solitude. In addition to scaring the animals out of their wits, the fireworks could also pose a threat of wildfire during a dry spell.

George Washington
National Forest

1. Big Schloss Area

The Big Schloss area, the northernmost part of the George Washington National Forest included in this guidebook, is located mainly in Shenandoah County, Virginia. A substantial fraction of the area covered in this chapter actually lies in West Virginia, but as it is all within the same national forest and forms one integral area, we include it here.

The region is generally steep and rugged, with many large rock outcrops that provide spectacular viewpoints above treetops. The most conspicuous of these formations is the Big Schloss itself, on the crest of Mill Mountain, but impressive outcrops exist at many other points. The area contains not only the usual southwest-to-northeast ridges—Mill Mountain and Little Sluice Mountain—but a perpendicular interconnecting ridge formed by Halfmoon Mountain and Sugar Knob.

The Big Schloss area probably was never settled. Iron ore was mined extensively throughout the area in the 1800s—long before the Forest Service even existed, let alone acquired the tract. You can find remains of this activity at Van Buren Furnace on County Road 713. Charcoal was produced from local timber to fuel the furnaces. Trees were cut in an area, then stacked in a small level circle and covered with earth. The wood burned with only small amounts of oxygen to form charcoal, which was then hauled off by horse and wagon to the furnace.

Timbering is still being practiced today at lower altitudes under the multiple-use concept. Clearcut patches, often quite large, can be seen from some points. The sections that have grown up for a few years may be worth exploring for types of wildlife that avoid heavy forest.

34

The tree cover is otherwise continuous except at rocky outcrops and a few grassy clearings maintained for the benefit of game. Most of the forest around the summit of Mill Mountain and some of the other high ridges contains a dense understory of mountain laurel. Off-trail travel in these areas consequently is strenuous.

Among wildflowers, the dwarf iris is notably common in late spring, growing in dry, sandy spots beside roads and trails.

Several developments exist in the area. The radio tower on the summit of Mill Mountain, and the power line that runs directly up the west side of the mountain to the tower are slated for removal by the Forest Service in the near future. Wolf Gap Campground offers limited car camping facilities, and the Potomac Appalachian Trail Club maintains a small stone cabin (locked) on the Little Stony Creek Trail near its junction with the Big Blue Trail.

Of great practical benefit to hikers and backpackers are several reliable springs at high elevations. Although there are no designated camping areas for backpackers within the "interior," suitable campsites can be found in a number of places.

All the trails described here except the lower portion of the Peer Trail are on public land. The Peer Trail is posted NO TRESPASSING, but there is an understanding between the owners and the Potomac Appalachian Trail Club, which maintains the trail, to let hikers walk along it. *Please follow the blazes carefully and stay on the trail.* Otherwise this privilege, which is not an official easement, may be revoked. It is for

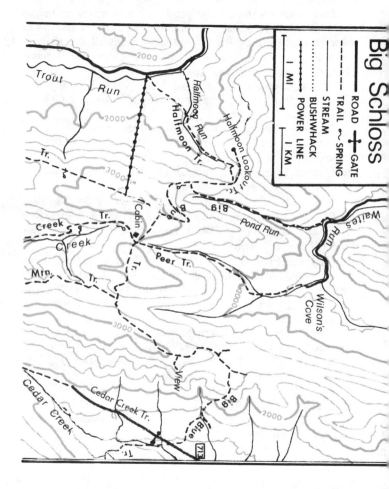

Big Schloss

—	ROAD	✝ GATE
– – –	TRAIL	∿ SPRING
———	STREAM	
··········	BUSHWHACK	
·+·+·+·	POWER LINE	

1 MI

1 KM

Trout Run

Halfmoon Run

Halfmoon Tr.

Halfmoon Lookout Tr.

Tr.

Creek Tr.

Creek

Cabin

Big Blue

Pond Run

Mtn. Tr.

Peer Tr.

Tr.

Waites Run

Wilson's Cove

View

Big Blue

Cedar Creek Tr.

Cedar Creek

Tr.

713

your own protection, too, as a fierce (biting!) dog guards the farm.

Trail names in the area depend on whose maps and signs you read. In particular, several trails have been linked together to form the "Big Blue Trail." Many of the signs at the trail junctions, however, still bear older trail names. Therefore, when referring to the Big Blue Trail, we also mention its alternate designations. The "Cut-off Trail" from FDR 92 to Wolf Gap Campground is not marked on Forest Service maps.

The Big Schloss area provides some excellent opportunities for circuit hikes, especially if you are willing to walk a couple of miles or so along lightly traveled Forest Development roads to complete the circuit. Some possibilities for such circuit hikes are:

(1) From Waites Run Road: Up and along the Big Blue Trail to the Peer Trail, down the Peer Trail to Waites Run Road, and back along Waites Run Road to the Big Blue Trail (11.9 km; 7.4 mi.).

(2) From FDR 88: Up the Little Sluice Mountain Trail, or the Bread Road and Little Sluice Mountain trails, along the Big Blue Trail, and back down the Cedar Run Trail to FDR 88 and your starting point (21.6 km or 17.2 km; 13.4 mi. or 10.7 mi.).

(3) From Wolf Gap Campground: Up Mill Mountain Trail past the Big Schloss, along the Big Blue Trail and down the Little Stony Creek Trail to FDR 92, along FDR 92, then back to the campground via either the Mill Creek and Mill Mountain trails or the abandoned Cut-off Trail (21.1 km; 13.1 mi.).

Maps: USGS Wardensville, Wolf Gap, and Woodstock quadrangles, 7.5 minute series.

MILL MOUNTAIN TRAIL

Length: 9.3 kilometers (5.8 miles)
Direction of travel: North
Difficulty: Moderate
Elevation: 686–1,003 meters (2,250–3,290 feet)
Difference in elevation: 317 meters (1,040 feet)
Markings: Yellow blazes
Trail # 1004

How to get there: Take County Road 675 west from Columbia Furnace to the Wolf Gap Campground (10.6 km; 6.6 mi.). The trail leaves near campsite #9.

The other end of the trail can be reached via the Big Blue Trail (Pond Run section).

Trail description: The trail climbs as a jeep road with several switchbacks, ascending 185 m (600 ft.) in 1.2 km (0.8 mi.). It passes close to but not over the wooded summit at the south end of Mill Mountain. The trail then decreases to a foot trail and proceeds northeast along the narrow ridge of the mountain.

About 50 m past the first rise, you will have some excellent views to the southeast. The trail mostly follows along the west side of the ridge below low rocky cliffs.

At 2.9 km (1.8 mi.) a side trail (white blazes) branches to the right, leading to the top of the ridge and then to the Big Schloss, the largest of the exposed rock formations in this area. After crossing a deep cleft in the rocks on a small wooden footbridge, the side trail ends on the bare rocks of the Big Schloss.

After the side trail branches off for the top of the Big Schloss, the main trail passes below the Big Schloss on the left. It follows the crest of the ridge, with superb views back and up at the Big Schloss.

A cairn marks the junction with the Mill Creek Trail (blazed blue), descending to the right at 3.7 km (2.3 mi.). The Mill Mountain Trail continues on straight ahead.

The trail hereafter proceeds slightly below the crest of the ridge, first mostly on the left and later mostly on the right. Occasional views may be obtained by scrambling up the rocky outcrops along the crest.

After crossing a rocky area at 6.4 km (4 mi.), the trail starts a steady moderate ascent and soon comes to Sandstone Spring (7 km; 4.4 mi.). The abundant clear water and the surrounding grove of hemlocks make this a popular—and often overcrowded—camping site.

Beyond this spot the trail runs very straight to the northeast, climbing at a moderate rate through a thick patch of mountain laurel. At 8.5 km (5.3 mi.) it passes within a few yards of the summit of Mill Mountain, where a radio tower is located.

The trail now descends moderately as a rough jeep trail, and at 9.3 km (5.8 mi.) it ends at the Big Blue Trail.

HALFMOON TRAIL

Length: 5.2 kilometers (3.2 miles)
Direction of travel: East
Difficulty: Moderate
Elevation: 488–953 meters (1,600–3,125 feet)
Difference in elevation: 465 meters (1,525 feet)
Markings: Yellow blazes
Trail # 1003
How to get there: From Columbia Furnace, go west on County Road 675, past Wolf Gap Campground. The trailhead is marked by a sign located at 9.7 km (6 mi.) beyond Wolf Gap. This is just at the point where a small power line starts straight up the side of Mill Mountain. This spot may also

be reached by driving 12.1 km (7.5 mi.) south from Wardensville, West Virginia, on Trout Run Road.

You can reach the opposite end of this trail via the Big Blue Trail.

Trail description: The Halfmoon Trail follows a woods road downhill and over a bridge across Trout Run. A gate blocks the road soon after the bridge.

Continuing on the other side of Trout Run as a woods road, the trail crosses an old overgrown power line clearing and climbs moderately, crossing several rivulets. At about 2.5 km (1.5 mi.), the trail traverses Halfmoon Run just below the junction of a side stream.

The woods road goes downhill from here, but the Halfmoon Trail turns right immediately after the crossing and climbs rather steeply as a foot trail, parallel to Halfmoon Run but well above it.

At one point the trail turns left, going steeply uphill for a few meters, and then turns right again, parallel to its original direction.

At 3.7 km (2.3 mi.) the trail enters a stony ravine and turns sharply right, then climbs steadily, curving to the left.

On the ridgetop, at 4.2 km (2.6 mi.), it joins the Halfmoon Lookout Trail (white blazes). The latter is 1.3 km (0.8 mi.) long, at first almost level but later starting a gradual ascent until close to its end, where it climbs very steeply to the viewpoint. Here you will find the stone foundations of an old lookout tower and an admirable view up the isolated Trout Run Valley.

At the junction with the trail to the lookout, the Halfmoon Trail turns right and climbs gently along a rounded ridgetop. At 5.2 km (3.2 mi.) the Halfmoon Trail ends at the intersection with the Big Blue Trail.

BIG BLUE TRAIL

Length: 14.6 kilometers (9.1 miles)
Direction of travel: Generally south and east
Difficulty: Strenuous
Elevation: 503–945–433 meters (1,650–3,100–1,420 feet)
Difference in elevation: 422-512 meters (1,450-1,680 feet)
Markings: Blue blazes
How to get there: Take Virginia Route 55 to Wardensville, West Virginia. In Wardensville, take Carpenter Avenue east for about 1.6 km (1 mi.) and turn right onto Waites Run Road just after passing the foot of a long hill and opposite a sign reading ALLEN HAWKINS COMMUNITY PARK. Go about 8.5 km (5.3 mi.) on Waites Run Road. The trail leaves from the right side of the road, just before the road crosses Waites Run. This section of the trail is also designated "Pond Run Trial."

The Big Blue Trail is a long side spur of the Appalachian trail and in most places is well maintained and marked. The Big Blue Trail largely follows sections of older trails which bear other names, and signs at trail junctions may indicate either name.

Trail description: The trail starts along the hillside with Pond Run on the left, then it crosses and follows the creek on the other side.

The trail ascends steadily, crossing Pond Run many times. Wading should not be necessary.

During our last visit to the area we found that trail maintenance was not up-to-date; a number of deadfalls required scrambling over, and the trail at times was obscured. These were minor obstacles, though, to an otherwise pleasant hike.

Numerous cascades and many large hemlocks make this section extremely attractive. One hemlock was found to be 3.4 m (11 ft) in circumference.

The trail now leaves the bottom of the ravine and climbs steeply up a rocky hillside to the right of the stream as a narrow and stony trail. It then climbs at a moderate to easy rate without crossing the stream.

Gradually the trail curves to the right of the ravine, becoming steeper, then climbing more gently. After passing through a fern glade at 3.2 km (2 mi.), it encounters the Halfmoon Trail coming in from the right. At this point the Big Blue Trail turns left.

After turning left, the trail crosses a small stream, the headwaters of Halfmoon Run, and shortly afterward passes near the spring that is its ultimate source.

A realigned section of the Big Blue Trail starts to ascend Mill Mountain toward the north. The trail here is a primitive foot path. After coming to an overlook into the clearings in Wilson's Cove, the trail turns back south, still climbing gently, to its junction with the Mill Mountain Trail. At this intersection the Big Blue Trail turns left and the Mill Mountain Trail runs straight ahead.

The Big Blue Trail continues as a jeep trail, passing many large anthills and descending through scrubby woods to a saddle at 6.3 km (3.9 mi.). At this point the Peer Trail leaves left and the Little Stony Creek Trail leaves right. A few meters down the Little Stony Creek Trail you will find the Sugar Knob Cabin and shortly afterward a spring.

From the saddle the Big Blue Trail goes straight ahead uphill and passes over a shoulder of Sugar Knob, with attractive open woods. It descends, at first moderately, later rather steeply, and at 7.8 km (4.8 mi.) meets the Little Sluice Mountain Trail coming in as a jeep trail from the right.

From this junction the Big Blue Trail first continues straight ahead as a foot trail and then turns to the left. It climbs at a moderate rate along the west side of Little Sluice

Mountain, passing a good viewpoint into Racer Camp Hollow on the left. It runs next along the broad ridge of the mountain, passing through scrubby oaks.

At 9.6 km (6 mi.), at a sign indicating VIEW 0.5 KM (0.3 MI.), a small trail (white blazes) winds downhill to the right to white rock cliffs with fine views first to the south and, at the end of the trail, to the north.

Shortly after the departure of this side trail, the Big Blue Trail passes a long low rocky wall on the left. It afterward briefly falls steeply from the top of the ridge, levels off again, and at 10.5 km (6.5 mi.) comes to a jeep trail.

Here the Big Blue Trail turns right along the jeep trail. Lupines grow in and near the trail at this point.

After roughly 0.6 km (0.4 mi.) on the jeep trail, the Big Blue Trail turns right as a foot trail, descending at an increasingly steep rate. The jeep trail continues straight ahead and ends at a recent clearcut. If you follow a logging road from the clearcut you will get to the four-way intersection mentioned at the beginning of the Cedar Creek Trail.

About 0.5 km (0.3 mi.) from the jeep trail, the Big Blue Trail bears left, while an abandoned trail drops steeply straight ahead.

The Big Blue Trail now goes steeply down a ridge and enters a broad dry ravine. The footpath is faint here, but the trail is well blazed.

The trail ascends slightly and then descends past large boulders into another ravine, which it follows downward.

After passing through a small clearing—a good campsite with water close by—the trail becomes much wider and runs beside a small stream on the right.

At 12.5 km (7.8 mi.) the Big Blue Trail turns right (*watch carefully for this*) and crosses the stream, while a wider trail goes straight ahead. This road leads to private land.

After fording the stream, the trail climbs the far bank and then drops gradually, skirting a grassy game clearing on the left. The trail now goes straight across a wide Forest Development Road. At 13.7 km (8.5 mi.) the trail turns right, upstream, beside Cedar Creek, which it soon crosses. After the crossing, which can be made on stones with care, the trail becomes muddy.

Shortly after reaching the end of a wet section the trail forks at 14.6 km (9.1 mi.). From this point the Big Blue Trail, the left fork, ascends Little North Mountain and follows its almost level ridge to the northeast, out of the Big Schloss area, and eventually reaches County Road 600 at Fetzer Gap.

The right fork is the Cedar Creek Trail, and leads to Forest Development Road 88.

PEER TRAIL

Length: 5.3 kilometers (3.3 miles)
Direction of travel: North
Difficulty: Easy
Elevation: 915–519 meters (3,000–1,700 feet)
Difference in elevation: 396 meters (1,300 feet)
Markings: Purple blazes
Trail # 1002
How to get there: Via the Big Blue Trail or, to hike the trail in the opposite direction from Wardensville, West Virginia, take Carpenter Avenue 1.6 km (1 mi.) and turn right onto Waites Run Road. Go 10.1 km (6.3 mi.) to the point where a large gate marks the beginning of private land. A few parking spaces are available just outside the gate.
Trail description: The Peer Trail starts from the Big Blue Trail in the saddle between Mill Mountain and Sugar Knob, opposite the trailhead for the Little Stony Creek Trail.

The trail descends steadily along the side of a ravine, well above Waites Run, which flows at the bottom. At first it is only a foot trail, but lower down it becomes an old unused woods road, wide and smooth.

The forest is attractive and open, with a mossy floor.

At 3 km (1.9 mi.), the trail approaches a large meadow on the right and skirts around two sides of it. A NO TRESPASSING sign will indicate the beginning of private land. The owners have privately agreed to let hikers cross it. Please stick closely to the blazed trail and avoid straying onto the rest of the property—their dog has been known to bite trespassers.

The trail goes along a dirt road, mostly through woods, and crosses a stream on a washed-out concrete bridge. At 4.2 km (2.6 mi.) it comes to another meadow with a shed for farm machinery. Here the trail (*watch the purple blazes*) leaves the road and turns right into the woods. Within 50 meters it meets a faint car track, and afterward turns left again.

The Peer Trail continues through woods. It then enters another meadow, skirting along the right edge—continue to watch for blazes.

After crossing a wooden bridge near a group of farm buildings, the trail joins a dirt road. It then crosses a concrete bridge and turns left to go through a gate onto Waites Run Road. At 5.3 km (3.3 mi.) it passes a large reservoir pond on the left.

Be sure to close all gates behind you so that farm animals will not wander away.

From the gate it is 1.6 km (1 mi.) left along Waites Run Road to the foot of the Big Blue Trail (Pond Run section).

MILL CREEK TRAIL

Length: 2.9 kilometers (1.8 miles)
Direction of travel: Northwest
Difficulty: Moderate
Elevation: 491–839 meters (1,610–2,750 feet)
Difference in elevation: 348 meters (1,140 feet)
Markings: Blue blazes
Trail # 415

How to get there: Via Forest Development Road 92 following directions to Little Stony Creek Trail. From Little Stony Creek, continue west on FDR 92 for 0.6 km (0.4 mi.). The trail leaves to the right, climbing up over the low road bank in the middle of a gentle curve to the right. The trailhead is marked by blue blazes on trees and rocks.

Trail description: The Mill Creek Trail climbs moderately as a woods road. It dips briefly and enters a broad rocky gully.

After crossing to the other side of the gully, the trail ascends more steeply below a giant stone wall. It follows a broad gently rounded ridge.

At 1.4 km (0.9 mi.), just after you have passed over the ridge, the trail makes a switchback and recrosses the ridge. It traverses a region of lichen-covered rocks.

The trail now enters a shallow ravine where the ground is covered with loose stones; then it switches back again.

Shortly after this second switchback, the rocks 30 m to the right of the trail offer a dramatic valley view.

At 2.1 km (1.3 mi.) the trail reaches the Mill Mountain Trail at the mountain's ridge. A small cairn marks the spot. From here it is about 0.8 km (0.5 mi.) south along the Mill Mountain Trail to the Big Schloss.

LITTLE STONY CREEK TRAIL

Length: 6 kilometers (3.7 miles)
Direction of travel: South
Difficulty: Moderate
Elevation: 915–397 meters (3,000–1,300 feet)
Difference in elevation: 518 meters (1,700 feet)
Markings: Yellow blazes
Trail # 571
How to get there: Via the Big Blue Trail. To hike the trail in a northerly direction, take County Road 675 west from Columbia Furnace for 0.8 km (0.5 mi.) and turn right onto County Road 608, which soon becomes Forest Development Road 88. At 3.7 km (2.3 mi.) turn left on FDR 92 and go 5.3 km (3.3 mi.) to the crossing of Little Stony Creek. The trail crosses the road there.
Trail description: The Little Stony Creek Trail starts on the Big Blue Trail at the saddle between Mill Mountain and Sugar Knob, opposite the Peer Trail.

About 50 m downhill, it passes the small Sugar Knob Cabin, which is maintained by the Potomac Appalachian Trail Club. The cabin is locked (for reservations see Introduction).

After another 50 m, the trail passes a spring on the left.

The trail descends beside the stream, crossing once after about 100 m and again after about 0.2 km (0.1 mi.). It then enters a field of rocks with an underground stream that is audible but usually not visible. The slope is entirely forested with relatively open woods.

Descending along the side of a steep hill, the trail passes another spring at 1.6 km (1 mi.).

Soon thereafter the trail's descent is moderated by two switchbacks. At the second switchback, the foot trail changes to a rough jeep trail, which after about 20 m crosses a small stream. After an additional 100 m it passes another spring.

Here the trail runs mostly about 100 m above Little Stony Creek, but later it descends to the stream, crossing a small tributary and passing in some places through dense growths of hemlock. It continues near the west bank of the stream until it crosses the Little Stony Creek Road, FDR 92, at 5.5 km (3.4 mi.) from the start.

On the other side of Little Stony Creek Road, the trail continues as a broad woods road. Within 100 m it crosses a small tributary of Little Stony Creek, followed by a slightly larger one called Mill Creek.

After crossing a third small stream, the trail makes a short and fairly steep descent and approaches Little Stony Creek. Here a side trail to the left leads to a beautiful view of the creek, with clear water flowing between mossy rocks, heavily shaded by large hemlocks.

At 6.9 km (4.3 mi.) a side road, which eventually becomes lost in the tangled vegetation, leaves to the right, and the Little Stony Creek Trail continues straight ahead.

The trail now passes an area of huge jumbled rocks on the right, with a small stream running beneath them. It then leads through a hemlock grove, with a side road branching left to the stream bank while the main trail continues to the right, passing below a high vertical cliff.

Soon hereafter, at 7.7 km (4.8 mi.), the trail reaches the Woodstock Reservoir. Beyond this point the trail leaves the national forest and enters private land. Please respect property rights and retrace your steps.

LITTLE SLUICE MOUNTAIN TRAIL

Length: 6.9 kilometers (4.3 miles)
Direction of travel: North
Difficulty: Moderate
Elevation: 476–820 meters (1,560–2,690 feet)
Difference in elevation: 344 meters (1,130 feet)
Markings: Purple blazes
Trail # 401

How to get there: From Columbia Furnace, take County Road 675 west about 0.8 km (0.5 mi.) to County Road 608, which leaves uphill to the right. Follow 608, which becomes Forest Development Road 88. At 3.7 km (2.3 mi.) FDR 92 leaves to the left. Continue straight ahead on FDR 88. The Little Sluice Mountain Trail begins on the left, 0.8 km (0.5 mi.) beyond the junction with FDR 92.

Reach the other end of the trail via the Big Blue Trail for a hike in the opposite direction.

Trail description: The Little Sluice Mountain Trail is a rough road, which first ascends at a moderate rate and at 0.5 km (0.3 mi.) from the trailhead turns right, climbing more steeply. At 1.4 km (0.9 mi.) from the start, the trail forks.

The right branch, which is 0.6 km (0.4 mi.) shorter, ascends along the side of the mountain, starting as a little-used jeep trail and later narrowing to a foot trail. Where this foot trail seems to diminish to nothing, the left fork of the trail can be rejoined by cutting through the woods to the ridgetop a few meters away.

From the fork the left branch of the trail ascends steeply via switchbacks to the summit ridge of Little Sluice Mountain. Where it reaches the summit, at 2.1 km (1.3 mi.), there is a grassy game clearing containing a few isolated spruces.

From this clearing a side trip south to the Little Schloss can be made. A trail has become established through frequent usage. Head straight across the meadow and into the woods on the opposite side, following the ridge crest to the southwest. Pass over one small rise, descend to a saddle, and then climb up to the large white cliffs of the Little Schloss, about 500 m after leaving the meadow. *Caution* is required because of many loose stones and rocks on the Little Schloss, but the views from the top are spectacular.

Returning to the meadow and rejoining the left fork of the Little Sluice Mountain Trail, you travel along the summit ridge of Little Sluice Mountain, almost level at first and then passing over a knob about 30 m high.

After descending the far side of this knob, the trail crosses a short level spot with large oak trees. Just where the trail curves to the left and starts downhill, at 3.4 km (2.1 mi.), you will see the Bread Road Trail leaving to the right.

After this junction, the Little Sluice Mountain Trail passes a clearing on the left, from which you obtain a nice view of the Big Schloss, 3.2 km (2 mi.) away as the crow flies but much farther as the hiker strides.

The trail then slowly descends the left flank of the ridge of Little Sluice Mountain. After passing over two saddles that join the main ridge to outlying knobs, a short side trail to the right leads to a spring at 5.3 km (3.3 mi.).

After crossing another saddle, the trail descends, turns left and then right, and crosses a stream that may run year-round.

The trail then ascends moderately until at 6.9 km (4.3 mi.) it ends at the Big Blue Trail.

BREAD ROAD TRAIL

Length: 1.6 kilometers (1 mile)
Direction of travel: West
Difficulty: Moderate
Elevation: 589–796 meters (1,930–2,610 feet)
Difference in elevation: 207 meters (680 feet)
Markings: Orange blazes
Trail # 411
How to get there: From Columbia Furnace take County Road 675 west for 0.8 km (0.5 mi.) and turn right onto County Road 608, which soon becomes Forest Development Road 88. Continue 3.4 km (2.1 mi.) on FDR 88 beyond its junction with FDR 92 and park at a small turnout just past the trailhead. You can reach the other end of the trail via the Little Sluice Mountain Trail.

Trail description: This trail, providing an alternate route to the top of Little Sluice Mountain, starts about 0.3 km (0.2 mi.) before the point where FDR 88 is chained off.

Follow a rough road about 60 paces uphill and, at the spot where it forks, curve around sharply to the left.

Continuing uphill on a moderate slope, the trail first is mossy, then becomes steeper and rougher. You may find water in the trail here after wet weather. This, together with a rocky and somewhat eroded trail, can make walking difficult, especially if you are trying to keep your feet dry.

The trail curves to the right and heads steeply up the hill, continuing through young trees and then entering older growth. The footing is poor, with loose stones on the steep slope, but the trail soon improves as it curves to the left and becomes less steep.

Finally it turns to the right and climbs again more steeply for about 100 m to Little Sluice Mountain Trail on the ridge of the mountain.

CEDAR CREEK TRAIL

Length: 5.1 kilometers (3.2 miles)
Direction of travel: Southwest
Difficulty: Easy
Elevation: 412–625 meters (1,350–2,050 feet)
Difference in elevation: 213 meters (700 feet)
Markings: Yellow blazes
Trail # 573

How to get there: From Van Buren Furnace or, to hike the trail in the opposite direction, from the end of Forest Development Road 88. To reach Van Buren Furnace from Columbia Furnace, go north 12.7 km (7.9 mi.) on County Road 623 to County Road 600 and turn left, crossing over North Mountain at Fetzer Gap. After 7.1 km (4.4 mi.) on 600, turn left on County Road 603 and go 1.9 km (1.2 mi.) to County Road 713. Continue straight on 713, pass the ruins of Van Buren Furnace, and enter the national forest where the road is gated. You will then come to what looks like a four-way intersection. The right turn leads to a recent clearcut, the left turn goes to Cedar Creek a few meters away and a gate. The road straight ahead is the beginning of the Cedar Creek Trail. You can either park here at the side of the road or continue straight ahead, past the junction with the Big Blue Trail, and park at a Forest Service gate.

To reach the end of FDR 88, go 0.8 km (0.5 mi.) west from Columbia Furnace on County Road 675 to County Road 608. Turn right on 608, which soon becomes FDR 88, and continue to its end. Here is a traffic circle type turnaround for your car.

Trail description: Walk up the road, past the point where the Big Blue Trail crosses it, and continue to follow it past the gate. It travels along a hillside a fair distance from Cedar

Creek itself, passing at one point over a small saddle. Some old mines can be seen in the hillside.

The trail was rerouted a while back because the old woods road beside the creek is often almost as wet as the creek itself. In fact, we once found the nest of a Louisiana waterthrush not in the bank of the creek, where it might be expected, but in the bank of the trail.

After keeping to the hillside for a while the trail approaches closer to the creek. Shortly thereafter it becomes a foot trail.

Continue following the yellow blazes. Eventually, the trail joins the old road next to Cedar Creek and follows it to the gate and the traffic circle on FDR 88 beyond.

If you do not mind possible wet feet, you can follow the Big Blue Trail down to the creek and hike up the old road beside it. The road is still easily followed, and you will eventually be joined by the actual trail, with its yellow blazes.

CUT-OFF TRAIL

Length: 0.6 kilometers (0.4 miles)
Direction of travel: Northwest
Difficulty: Moderate
Elevation: 549–650 meters (1,800–2,130 feet)
Difference in elevation: 101 meters (330 feet)
Markings: None
How to get there: The base of the trail is located on Forest Development Road 92, 4.5 km (2.8 mi.) west of the point where the road crosses Little Stony Creek. The trail starts up the hillside just where the road begins to run slightly downhill into a ravine, where it makes a switchback.
Trail description: This trail, once it's found, is easily followed, as it is an old roadbed cut deeply into the hillside.

The trail has been unmaintained in recent years, but vegetation has not yet totally reclaimed it.

The ascent toward County Road 675 is quite steep, and the trail meets 675 just below Wolf Gap Campground.

2. Laurel Fork Area

The Laurel Fork area is a high-altitude region in the northwestern corner of Highland County, bordered on the north and west by West Virginia. The Laurel Fork, the stream that gives the region its name, flows from south to north, bisecting it. In the eastern section is Middle Mountain, a narrow ridge that parallels the Laurel Fork. The western section consists of fingerlike ridges that point toward the Laurel Fork. Between these ridges, six tributaries flow eastward into the main stream, and trails follow four of them. The main attraction of the area is its relative remoteness and gentle beauty.

Around the turn of the century the land in the Laurel Fork area was owned by the Norfolk & Western Railroad. The company logged it and hauled the timber out via narrow-gauge railroads that ran along the slopes above the streams. The tract was burned, too, some time after the logging. The railbeds, stripped of hardware, still exist, and their gentle grades form the basis of much of the trail system.

The U.S. Forest Service purchased the land in 1922. Since then the forest has regenerated, with only a modest amount of thinning being done by the agency. It now is a fine example of a young northern hardwood forest.

At almost all headwaters you can find beaver ponds and meadows. In fact, you can't miss them! Dawn and dusk are good times to watch beavers at work. If you are lucky, you may see a snowshoe hare, mink, or muskrat. Streams are stocked with brook trout and support some native trout.

The trees most commonly seen are red spruce, hemlock, white pine, and red maple at high elevations, and northern red oak, sugar maple, beech, yellow and sweet (black) birch, and black cherry throughout the rest of the area. Rhododendron and mountain laurel are most conspicuous close

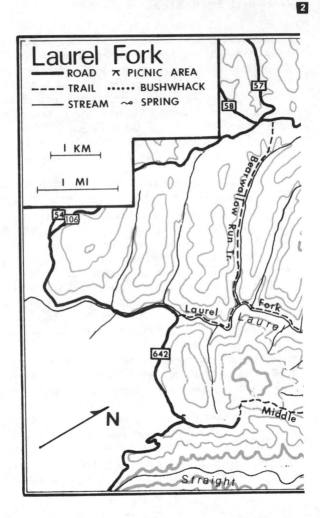

2

Laurel Fork

- —— ROAD
- ---- TRAIL
- —— STREAM
- ✕ PICNIC AREA
- ...... BUSHWHACK
- ~ SPRING

1 KM

1 MI

57

58

54 106

Bearwallow Run Tr.

Laurel   Laure   Fork

642

N

Middle

Straight

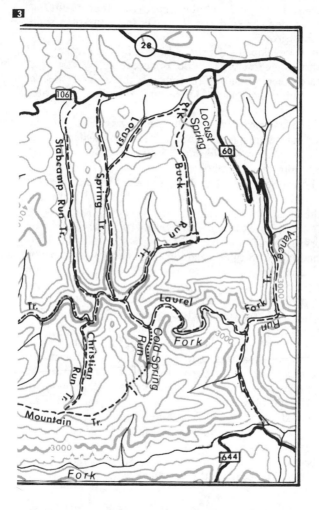

to the Laurel Fork. Greenbrier, wintergreen, aster, golden-rod, mosses, ferns, and an abundance of other plants, as well as mushrooms, round out the inventory. In some spots berry bushes grow.

The only developed campsite is Locust Spring Picnic Area, in the northern corner. This site is accessible by dirt road and features picnic tables, fire rings, a three-sided shelter, a spring, and vault toilets. There are abundant campsites along the Laurel Fork.

The beaver meadows in the upper reaches of the tributaries are tempting campsites. They are fragile and get trampled easily, however, besides often being wet, so try to find a campsite in the woods instead.

The Forest Service claims there are 45.9 kilometers (28.5 miles) of trails in the Laurel Fork area. But most trails are, to say the least, informal. That's all right, as long as you are forewarned to expect a little bushwhacking. The forest understory is sparse, and bushwhacking is not difficult. Only in the rhododendron thickets along the Laurel Fork can you get really tangled up if you lose the trail. But even they are manageable with a few short detours.

Most of the trailheads and junctions are well marked. In between the markers, you need imagination. The Forest Service has done very little trail work, while the beavers have done quite a lot. Trails in the upper reaches of the tributaries near the beaver meadows tend to meander and disappear. The best procedure seems to be to stick fairly close to the hillsides while bypassing the beaver ponds and to look for game trails and railroad grades that are going your way. This has the added advantage of lessening human impact on the meadows. Carry a topographic map and keep your eye on the ridgetops and streams as landmarks.

Farther down the tributaries, the valleys narrow, the beaver ponds disappear, and you can pick up a real trail or railroad grade that leads to the bottom. The old railroad grades make excellent trails when they go where you want to go. Many of them, however, tend to creep higher and higher on the hillsides or even to disappear. The solution, then, is to bushwhack down to the nearest stream, where you usually can find a fisherman's trail, a game trail, or another railroad grade.

The trail along the Laurel Fork is good, but it crosses the stream a number of times. Upstream, wading is not necessary, except perhaps when the water is very high. Downstream from the Slabcamp Run Trail junction, it is necessary to wade across.

The Laurel Fork Trail and the Middle Mountain Trail cross private land for short distances (see trail descriptions). Be considerate and don't abuse the privilege of passage. All other trails are on public land.

The Laurel Fork area offers many possibilities for circuit hikes. All trails in the western section are connected at the top by Forest Development Road 106 and at the bottom by the Laurel Fork Trail. The shortest circuit, Buck Run to Locust Spring, is about 9.7 kilometers (6 miles) long, starting and ending at the Locust Spring Picnic Area. For most other circuits you will have to walk along FDR 106 or FDR 60 for part of the way, and that can be somewhat boring. But you should examine the map and make up your own circuit hike.

The Locust Spring Picnic Area is a good starting point from which to reach the trails. To get to the picnic area from the south, go west from Monterey on U.S. 250 for 33.8 kilometers (21 miles) and turn sharply right onto West Virginia Route 28. Go 10.8 kilometers (6.7 miles) and turn right onto a dirt road marked LOCUST SPRING PICNIC AREA. Turn left at the first intersection (Allegheny Road—FDR 106—goes right). Bear right at the second intersection (FDR 60 goes left) to the picnic ground.

From the north, take U.S. 33 west from Harrisonburg through Franklin, West Virginia. At 22.5 kilometers (14 miles) past Franklin, turn left onto West Virginia Route 28. From there it is 25.7 kilometers (16 miles) to the turnoff on the left marked LOCUST SPRING PICNIC AREA. Follow above directions to the picnic area.

Maps: USGS Thornwood and Snowy Mountain quadrangles, 7.5 minute series; Warm Springs Ranger District map, George Washington National Forest.

LAUREL FORK TRAIL

Length: 14.5 kilometers (9 miles)
Direction of travel: Generally south
Difficulty: Moderate to easy
Elevation: 904–970 meters (2,965 –3,180 feet)
Difference in elevation: 66 meters (215 feet)
Markings: Blue blazes
Trail # 450
How to get there: From the Locust Spring Picnic Area, take Forest Development Road 60 downhill, via switchbacks, to the point where it ends beside Vance Run. The trail runs from there down Vance Run.

If you wish to hike the trail in the opposite direction, go south on FDR 106 to its junction with County Road 642 and turn left. At 1.6 km (1 mi.) after 642 crosses the Laurel Fork, a dirt road turns back on the left, with a marker for the Laurel Fork Trail. Park on County Road 642 and do not drive down the dirt road, which leads to private property.

Trail description: The trail, an old woods road closed to motorized vehicles, follows Vance Run east through thick woods. It descends gently in the steep-sided valley.

At the confluence of Vance and Sam's runs, the trail turns south; a little later it returns east.

At 2.4 km (1.5 mi.) Vance Run flows into the Laurel Fork. (The old woods road continues downstream 1.9 km [1.2 mi.] along the Laurel Fork to meet a road at the confluence of the Laurel Fork and Straight Fork. Beyond this point, the river is called the North Fork of the South Branch of the Potomac River.)

Back at the place where Vance Run flows into the Laurel Fork, turn right (south) onto the actual trail along the Laurel Fork. The trail is now a footpath, following the Laurel Fork upstream. It is rather level and easy hiking, but be prepared to wade across the stream on numerous occasions.

Shortly after you have begun hiking up the Laurel Fork, you will come to a beautiful cliff rising straight up out of the river on the left bank.

In a few places the trail is overgrown with rhododendrons, but this is nothing to worry about. You can still follow the path through the thickets by bending over a little and parting the branches with your hands.

You will find some grassy clearings beside the river. In a few, old apple trees are growing. The fruit is small and a bit on the sour side, but you may enjoy picking and eating some anyway during the fall.

The Laurel Fork has attractive swimming holes in a few places. Occasional rocky bluffs make for scenic hiking.

At 6 km (3.7 mi.) you will see Cold Spring Run joining the Laurel Fork on the left. Shortly thereafter, Buck Run flows into the river on the right. From here the trail will be quite obvious—again an old woods road—and the stream crossings usually can be negotiated without wading, although conditions vary with the water level.

A good number of streams flow into the Laurel Fork at short intervals, with trails following most of them. Some intervals, from stream to stream, are:

Cold Spring Run to Buck Run	1.1 km (0.7 mi.)
Buck Run to Locust Spring Run	0.5 km (0.3 mi.)
Locust Spring Run to Slabcamp Run	0.5 km (0.3 mi.)
Slabcamp Run to Christian Run	0.8 km (0.5 mi.)
Christian Run to Bearwallow Run	3.9 km (2.4 mi.)

The Laurel Fork Trail winds its way along the river valley, always staying close to the stream. The turns and twists are quite scenic, and the hiking is easy.

At 12.7 km (7.9 mi.), near the confluence of Laurel Fork and Bearwallow Run, there is a flat open area with a beaver pond right on the Laurel Fork. Some of it has become meadowlike but is still rather soggy. Tread carefully if you venture here, or you will have wet feet in no time. The beaver dam was in good repair when we were there last.

At 14.3 km (8.9 mi.) you will reach the end of the national forest property. Cross the stream for the last time, and you will find a cabin on your left. The land around it is privately owned, but the Forest Service has an agreement with the owners whereby they permit access to the Laurel Fork. Make sure you stay on the dirt road and do not stray onto the private property. If the access privilege is abused, it will be revoked.

The trail ends at 14.5 km (9 mi.) on County Road 642.

BUCK RUN TRAIL

Length: 4 kilometers (2.5 miles)
Direction of travel: Southeast
Difficulty: Moderate
Elevation: 869–1,159 meters (2,850–3,800 feet)

Difference in elevation: 290 meters (950 feet)
Markings: Blue blazes
Trail # 598
How to get there: The trail starts at the Locust Spring Picnic Area. The other end of the trail can be reached via the Laurel Fork Trail.
Trail description: Buck Run Trail begins just east of the parking area for the Locust Spring Picnic Area. Bear right on a gated two-track trail, which may have been an old railroad grade or logging road. Follow it for about 0.8 km (0.5 mi.) through woods along the side of a hill. To your left (north) you will see beaver ponds and meadows.

In a low saddle, just past a good view of beaver ponds, the trail forks. Take the left branch—not too obvious—down through open woods toward the stream.

Going downhill from the saddle, the trail meanders along the edge of more beaver ponds, and among meadows and spruces. You can see a lot of birds here.

Eventually the trail merges with another railroad grade that comes in from the right (south). Follow this grade for 1.3 km (0.8 mi.) along the north side of Buck Knob. Buck Run drops farther below to your left.

Just before you reach the eastern end of Buck Knob, where the railroad grade turns the corner to the right, the trail forks again. The Buck Run Trail goes left as a narrow footpath, dropping off the railroad grade and descending by switchbacks to Buck Run. This split from the railroad grade is ill-defined, but there is a forked tree in the middle of the division. If you notice the railroad grade turning right (south) around the end of Buck Knob, you have gone about 30 m too far.

At the bottom of the switchbacks, the trail crosses Buck Run to the north side, follows the bank for a short distance, and then recrosses to the south bank at the spot where the stream turns southward. These are the only stream crossings along this trail, and they do not require wading.

From the second crossing of Buck Run, it is 1.9 km (1.2 mi.) to the Laurel Fork. The trail follows the west bank, remaining close to Buck Run. You will find a trail marker at the junction with the Laurel Fork Trail, only a short distance from the Laurel Fork. There are a number of good campsites nearby.

LOCUST SPRING TRAIL

Length: 5.6 kilometers (3.5 miles)
Direction of travel: Southeast
Difficulty: Moderate
Elevation: 873–1,159 meters (2,862–3,800 feet)
Difference in elevation: 286 meters (938 feet)
Markings: Blue blazes
Trail #s 633 and 633A
How to get there: This trail has two trailheads. Approach 1, which is the easier to follow, begins at the Locust Spring Picnic Area. Approach 2, which requires a bit more imagination, begins at Forest Development Road 106, 2.1 km (1.3 mi.) south of the road to the picnic area. A sign marks the spot.

You can reach the opposite end of the trail via the Laurel Fork Trail.

Trail description: For Approach 1: Walk from the Locust Spring Picnic Area toward the spring and you will see the trailhead to your left, before you drop down to the spring. The trail is *not* open to motorized vehicles of any kind, including trail bikes.

For 1.3 km (0.8 mi.) the trail is easy to follow, leading through hemlocks and white pines, most of which obviously have been planted. Then it forks, the right branch going down to Locust Spring Run. Take the narrower left branch through more evergreen forest. The trail eventually drops down to the stream and crosses it several times. Continue through open, not-too-brushy bottomland, crossing and recrossing the stream.

Near a stand of red pine on the hill to your left (northeast), you will come to the junction with the other approach to Locust Spring Trail. Cross to the south side of the stream.

For Approach 2: Leave FDR 106 and head down through the woods for 50 m until you reach Locust Spring Run. Keep generally to the right (south) of the creek.

After following the stream for 150 m you will begin to encounter a series of beaver ponds. Keep to the south of them, following the trail or game trails, or bushwhacking, as necessary. At the bottom of the chain of beaver ponds is a marshy area, from which the trail eventually emerges. It becomes a railroad grade along the south side of the stream.

Look for a valley coming in from the north and the junction with Approach 1 to Locust Spring Trail at 2.7 km (1.7 mi.).

After the junction, the combined trails follow the railroad grade intermittently. The path crosses the stream several times, but no wading is necessary. The forest is open.

After the final stream crossing, the valley narrows. The trail becomes a railroad grade, following the north bank of the stream for the remaining distance.

You will find a trail marker at the end of the trail, near the Laurel Fork. Just to the south is a fire ring. Many good campsites are available.

SLABCAMP RUN TRAIL

Length: 4 kilometers (2.5 miles)
Direction of travel: Southeast
Difficulty: Moderate
Elevation: 885–1,113 meters (2,900–3,650 feet)

Difference in elevation: 228 meters (750 feet)
Markings: Blue blazes
Trail # 600
How to get there: Go south on Forest Development Road 106 for 2.7 km (1.7 mi.) past the road to the Locust Spring Picnic Area and park near the sign marking the trailhead.

The opposite end of the trail can be reached via the Laurel Fork Trail.

Trail description: The trail forks 30 m from the trailhead; take the right fork and follow it down a gentle hill. You will pass a roadblock.

The trail levels off, winding through a meadow and skirting the inevitable series of beaver ponds. It then narrows to a foot trail and becomes rather difficult to follow.

Once past the beaver ponds, the trail follows Slabcamp Run and crosses it numerous times. Be on the alert! Much of the best trail is on the north side of the stream, but it runs up and down the side of the hill. In many places it hardly seems to exist. For the last kilometer (0.6 mi.) you will probably have to walk down the broad, gently sloping streambed. No difficulties here, except during high water.

There are some interesting rock formations along the way, green and gray sandstone and shale. This is a good place for rock hounds to stop for a look around.

At trail's end, the junction with the Laurel Fork Trail is marked by a sign.

To reach the main part of the Laurel Fork Trail, you must cross to the east side of the Laurel Fork, and wading probably will be necessary.

BEARWALLOW RUN TRAIL

Length: 4 kilometers (2.5 miles)
Direction of travel: Southeast
Difficulty: Moderate

Elevation: 961–1,129 meters (3,150–3,700 feet)
Difference in elevation: 168 meters (550 feet)
Markings: Blue blazes
Trail # 601
How to get there: Take Forest Development Road 106 south for 6.3 km (3.9 mi.) past the road to the Locust Spring Picnic Area and park at the sign marking the trailhead.

You can reach the opposite end of the trail via the Laurel Fork Trail.

Trail description: From the trailhead, follow the trail until it disappears into beaver ponds and meadows along Bearwallow Run.

Here you will have to be a little ingenious to avoid wet feet. Your best strategy is to stay to the right (south) of the beaver ponds, keeping low on the side of the hill. Follow game trails and old logging or railroad grades wherever possible. Expect to do some bushwhacking.

The scenic views redeem this trail. There are beautiful vistas over open meadows with ferns and scattered spruces. It's worth the scrambling.

About 1.6 km (1 mi.) down the valley, on the south side in a stand of hemlocks, you will arrive at a good railroad grade. It can be followed the rest of the way down Bearwallow Run to the Laurel Fork.

The trail junction with the Laurel Fork Trail is marked by a signpost near the Laurel Fork. There are good campsites nearby.

MIDDLE MOUNTAIN TRAIL

Length: 4.3 kilometers (2.7 miles)
Direction of travel: Northeast
Difficulty: Easy to moderate
Elevation: 1,154–1,190 meters (3,784–3,901 feet)
Difference in elevation: 36 meters (117 feet)

Markings: Blue blazes

Trail # 457

How to get there: From the Locust Spring Picnic Area, drive south on Forest Development Road 106 to its junction with Country Road 642. Turn left on 642, which goes downhill, crosses the Laurel Fork, and climbs Middle Mountain. At the top of the mountain, the road turns sharply right. On the left is a dirt road and a sign pointing left toward the Middle Mountain Trail. Drive up the dirt road—not the private driveway to the left of it—for 1.1 km (0.7 mi.) and park in the small parking area.

Trail description: The Middle Mountain Trail begins at the gate to the meadow on the west. You will be walking on private land for 0.5 km (0.3 mi.) until you pass another gate. Please respect your access privilege!

One hundred meters beyond this gate, turn sharply right onto a somewhat washed-out dirt road, which goes uphill in a sweeping curve across an open field or meadow. After 200 m on this road and immediately beside it, there is a large rounded rock pile, 3 m high and 6 m wide at its base. A hundred meters beyond this rock pile is a wood, a fence, a gate, and a Forest Service sign. Behind this gate the trail continues on public land.

Follow the old jeep road into the woods. The trail then goes downhill, passing a road going off to the left (west). Here you will find a large stand of hemlocks.

The trail now generally follows the ridgeline, with ups and downs of a few hundred meters. There are several logging roads on the left (west). Ignore them.

At 2.7 km (1.7 m.) from the car, in an open area at the bottom of a downhill stretch, you will reach a fork where the Christian Run Trial drops off to the west. This junction makes a good campsite, but the nearest water is 1.3 km (0.8 mi.) away, down Christian run trail.

Past this junction, the Middle Mountain Trail narrows at a log gate and becomes strictly a footpath. It follows the ridgetop uphill for 0.8 km (0.5 mi.) to a level area and a Y in the trail. The left branch of the Y peters out in a little while.

Taking the right branch of the Y, down the east side of the ridge, you will look northwest into the drainage of Cold Spring. Here you will have to make a choice: either return the way you came, or bushwhack down the ridge via Cold Spring Run to the Laurel Fork.

COLD SPRING RUN: This is not a trail, so follow directions carefully and, if possible, use a topographic map and compass.

Leave Middle Mountain Trail 0.8 km (0.5 mi.) past the Y at the point where the trail turns sharply right, and angle down the slope, going north. About 0.3 km (0.2 mi.) below is the source of Cold Spring Run.

Find the creek and follow it downstream to the Laurel Fork. It is 1.9 km (1.2 mi.) from where you left the Middle Mountain Trail to the Laurel Fork, and the bushwhacking is fairly easy.

At the bottom you should arrive at the Laurel Fork Trail, which will take you south up the Laurel Fork to Buck Run and the other trail junctions. It is 1.1 km (0.7 mi.) from Cold Spring Run to Buck Run. You will have to wade, crossing the Laurel Fork opposite Buck Run.

CHRISTIAN RUN TRAIL

Length: 2.6 kilometers (1.6 miles)
Direction of travel: Northwest
Difficulty: Easy
Elevation: 1,144–900 meters (3,750–2,950 feet)
Difference in elevation: 244 meters (800 feet)
Markings: Intermittent blue blazes

Trail # 599

How to get there: The Christian Run Trail begins 2.7 km (1.7 mi.) from the beginning of the Middle Mountain Trail. The opposite end of the trail can be reached by following the Laurel Fork Trail.

Trail description: The trail, a grassy track, starts at a beautiful meadow on the west slope of Middle Mountain. You will probably lose the trail in the summer in the high grass. Pick it up again farther downhill, where the trail entering the woods becomes evident.

After a very short time, if it is summer, you may encounter waist-high nettles, so you should be wearing long pants and a shirt or sweater for protection. You can lift your arms above the sea of nettles.

As you proceed downhill, the nettles eventually disappear. When they no longer hold your attention, you will notice you are entering a beautiful stand of hemlocks. Christian Run bubbles on your left at some distance from the trail.

Follow the trail downstream to the Laurel Fork. A trail marker indicates the junction with the Laurel Fork Trail.

3. Ramsey's Draft Wilderness

The Ramsey's Draft area is located in Augusta and Highland counties. The land around Ramsey's Draft itself was one of the first tracts to be acquired by the U.S. Forest Service when George Washington National Forest was established. No settlers ever lived in the steep, narrow valley, for they would have been unable to carve out a living. There is practically no flat terrain along Ramsey's Draft that would lend itself to building a house and a garden, let alone farming. But the remains of a pioneer settlement, including an old cemetery, can be found at Puffenbarger Pond, near where Forest Development Road 95 crosses Shenandoah Mountain. Some inscriptions on the stones marking the graves can still be deciphered.

The parallel ridges of Shenandoah Mountain on the west and Bald Ridge on the east plus a connecting ridge form a roughly horseshoe-shaped mountain; the terrain within the horseshoe is drained by Ramsey's Draft. The exterior slope of the horseshoe lies in several other watersheds, namely Shaw Fork on the west, the Calfpasture River on the east, and the North River on the north.

The distance between Shenandoah Mountain and Bald Ridge is about 4 kilometers (2.5 miles) as the crow flies. These ridges rise approximately 300 meters (1,000 feet) above the valley floor. The terrain is characterized by steep slopes almost everywhere except near the eastern perimeter.

There are pockets of virgin forest in Ramsey's Draft—a rarity in the central Appalachians. Perhaps as much as 24.3 square kilometers (6,000 acres) never have been subjected to the axe and chain saw. The huge hemlocks, white pines, oaks, and yellow poplars are in remarkable contrast to smaller trees found nearby.

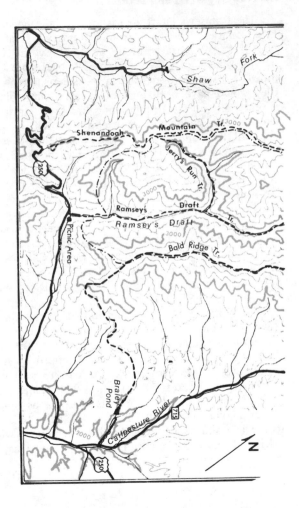

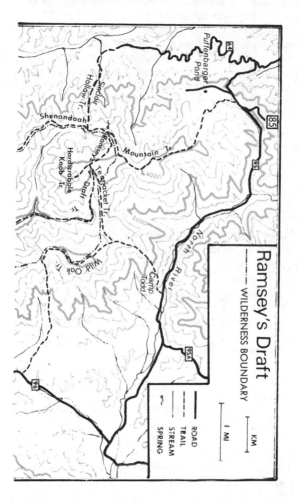

Ramsey's Draft

— WILDERNESS BOUNDARY

ROAD
TRAIL
STREAM
SPRING

KM
MI

Puffenbarger Pond

Cedar Hollow Tr.

Shenandoah

Hardscrabble Knob Tr.

Ramsey's Draft

Tearjacket Tr.

Mountain Tr.

4000

3000

North River

Camp Todd

Wild Oak Tr.

You can experience a sensation of true wilderness in the hemlock forests along the upper prongs of Ramsey's Draft, where there is a deeply shaded understory of moss and ferns. In other places the forest has different aspects. On some mountain ridges the forest floor is carpeted with grass, and in some steep ravines large trees grow directly out of stony slopes that seem almost devoid of soil cover. Azaleas and mountain laurel are common. Small wildflowers are abundant, especially before trees come into full foliage in the spring.

Hunters in great numbers are attracted during hunting season. If you plan a hike at that time, wear something bright and be noisy—talk, sing, or whistle so there will be no mistake about your species identity. Or stay home altogether.

Ravens and pileated woodpeckers are among the more noticeable birds. Breeding birds include several northern species which find suitable habitats in the dense virgin hemlock forests, such as the winter wren and the Canada and blackburnian warblers.

An area measuring 27.1 square kilometers (6,700 acres) within Ramsey's Draft was designated a wilderness by Congress. Although it protects the horseshoe-shaped valley and the virgin forests, this area includes only the interior sides of the valley up to the ridgetops of the surrounding mountains.

On the eastern side of Bald Ridge there are a number of old jeep trails, which start from Augusta County Road 715. Many just peter out once they reach the steeper slopes of the mountain, generally at an elevation of around 760 meters (2,500 feet). One road, however, leads to the picnic area at Braley Pond, which is an artificial impoundment. This road, paved at its beginning, leaves Augusta County Road 715 about 0.6 km (0.4 mi.) north of U.S. 250. From the picnic area, a trail on the right side of the pond will guide you to the start of the Bald Ridge Trail.

Camping spots are numerous along the outer perimeter of the Ramsey's Draft area, especially along Forest Development roads 95 and 96. The water of the North River constitutes part of the water supply for Staunton. The riverbanks have been protected against erosion by gabions—medium-sized stones piled high and held in place by wire mesh.

There is a picnic area beside U.S. 250 at the beginning of the Ramsey's Draft Trail, but no camping is permitted there. There are many good camping spots along the Ramsey's Draft Trail. Whenever possible, try to use the established campsites, with their fire rings, rather than building new ones.

Ramsey's Draft Trail has many fords. A few can be crossed dry-footed, but for others wading is the only choice, so plan on wet feet.

A new trail connecting Bald Ridge Trail with Ramsey's Draft Trail near the Mountain House Picnic Area off U.S. Route 250 was in the early construction stage when we investigated it. Watch for markers pointing to this trail sometime in the future.

Maps: USGS West Augusta, Palo Alto, and McDowell quadrangles, 7.5 minute series; Ramsey's Draft Wilderness map, George Washington National Forest.

SHENANDOAH MOUNTAIN TRAIL

Length: 17.2 kilometers (10.7 miles)
Direction of travel: Generally north
Difficulty: Moderate
Elevation: 890–1,244–915 meters (2,920–4,080–3,000 feet)
Difference in elevation: 354–329 meters (1,160–1,080 feet)
Markings: Blue blazes
Trail # 447

How to get there: The trailhead is at a scenic turnout on U.S. 250, 26.9 km (16.7 mi.) west of Churchville. Approached from the west, the turnout is 29 km (18 mi.) from Monterey on U.S. 250. Park at the turnout.

This is a one-way trail, so you will need a car shuttle at the end. To get to the termination of the trail, if you are coming from Churchville, turn off U.S. 250 to the right immediately after passing the bridge over the Calfpasture River. You will then be on County Road 715. (Coming from Monterey, the turnoff is just before the bridge and to the left.) The pavement of 715 ends at 5.3 km (3.3 mi.), and the road becomes Forest Development Road 96. At 10 km (6.2 mi.) FDR 96 joins FDR 95. Turn left onto FDR 95. At 21.7 km (13.5 mi.), 250 m (550 ft.) after you pass FDR 85 entering from the north, the Shenandoah Mountain trailhead is on the left. A small opening in the woods marks the trail's beginning.

Trail description: The trail starts on the northwest side of the turnout on U.S. 250. After entering the trail beyond the retaining wall at the parking lot, turn right to follow the trail (straight ahead is a somewhat washed-out gully from the top of the hill—this is *not* the trail). After a few meters you will come to a junction: on the left is a shorter trail going steeply up the hill; straight ahead lies a longer, more gentle ascent. These two trails actually form the circuit hike of the Confederate Breastworks—a walk of about thirty to forty-five minutes. The actual Shenandoah Mountain Trail starts where these two trails meet again, just behind the top of the hill, and follows the side of the mountain to the left (west). The walking becomes easy at this point.

The trail continues winding its way through open woods along the ridge of Shenandoah Mountain, with only very minor ups and downs. At times you will find nice views, especially during the winter months after the leaves have fallen.

Just before the junction with Jerry's Run Trail at 4.3 km (2.7 mi.), you will enter the wilderness area, marked with a sign and trail register. Jerry's Run Trail branches off to the right. Down it, the former site of Sexton Cabin is 0.7 km (0.4 mi.) distant, and Ramsey's Draft Trail 3.2 km (2 mi.). A trail on the left to Shaw Fork has practically vanished due to lack of use. The land along Shaw Fork is privately owned, and you should not trespass.

The Shenandoah Mountain Trail continues level near the ridge of Shenandoah Mountain for slightly more than 8 km (5 mi.), through woods. On the east side of the ridge it passes through an open forest of sometimes very large hardwoods, whereas on the more steeply sloping west side of the ridge it leads through scrubby oaks and pines, with an understory of mountain laurel. At 11.6 km (7.2 mi.) you will meet a fork in the trail: Stay to the right. Before long the trail passes through a grassy clearing, where you will find a wilderness boundary sign and a trail register. From this clearing the Sinclair Hollow Trail leaves to the left and descends the west side of the mountain. The first 100 m are very faint. The Shenandoah Mountain Trail continues straight ahead past the clearing.

At 12.6 km (7.8 mi.) you will arrive at the upper end of the Ramsey's Draft Trail. It runs into the Shenandoah Mountain Trail from the right (east) in a small saddle with an open forest of very large trees. Six small evergreens, about 1 m apart in a straight line, make a good landmark at this point. A spring, which is dry in late summer, can be found a few meters down the west slope of the mountain, opposite Ramsey's Draft Trail.

The Shenandoah Mountain Trail now passes along the west slope of several knobs and at 15.4 km (9.6 mi.) from the trailhead the path begins to drop downhill at a moderate rate. There are some excellent views here looking northwest down a wooded valley, past Puffenbarger Pond and Meadows, into West Virginia's Pendleton County.

Continue hiking downhill. At 16.6 km (10.3 mi.) you will reach a small grassy meadow. On the west side of this clearing is a narrow, unmarked deer trail that leads sharply downhill toward Puffenbarger Pond. It soon vanishes completely, but by following the ridge downhill through the woods one eventually encounters the old meadows and apple trees that remain from early settlers in this area. This route is for the adventurous only!

The Shenandoah Mountain Trail leaves the meadow on the opposite side, bears sharply east, and then continues downhill. Following it, you will cross a small creek at 17.2 km (10.7 mi.) and arrive at FDR 95.

RAMSEY'S DRAFT TRAIL

Length: 11.3 kilometers (7 miles)
Direction of travel: Generally north and west
Difficulty: At first level and easy, except in flood-affected regions; later steep and more strenuous
Elevation: 687–1,232 meters (2,252–4,040 feet)
Difference in elevation: 545 meters (1,788 feet)
Markings: None, but trail is mostly easy to follow
Trail # 440
How to get there: Drive west on U.S. 250 from Churchville to the Mountain House Picnic Area on the right at 23.5 km (14.6 mi.). From the picnic area, take the road across a small concrete bridge to the rear parking area. Ramsey's Draft Trail starts as a continuation of the entrance road, beyond the parking area. The other end of the trail can be reached via the Shenandoah Mountain Trail.

Trail description: In 1985, a week of heavy rains caused a flood that tore out large sections of Ramsey's Draft Trail, which previously had been an easy-to-follow woods road. Now only bits and pieces of the road are left, and at times you will be on your own to find your way across or along the side of the stream. You cannot get lost because the steep mountains on either side of Ramsey's Draft will keep you on course.

There are many logjams and parts of washed-out concrete from the fords of the old road. You can usually find your way over and around them by following footpaths of varying distinctness, unless another flood just washed them out. Then you are on your own.

The difficulty of the stream crossings will vary greatly with the seasons: In late summer Ramsey's Draft flows mostly under the gravel left by the flood, and it appears dry except where the water flows over exposed bedrock. In the spring, the water may be sufficiently deep, cold, and fast-moving to make the crossings difficult and uncomfortable.

The narrow valley is densely wooded and some magnificent large trees can be found. In many places the forest floor beneath these trees is deeply shaded and free of undergrowth. Here you can find many fine campsites with established fire rings.

At 3.4 km (2.1 mi.) Jerry's Run joins Ramsey's Draft, just at the end of an especially long and severe flood washout of the woods road. Shortly afterward Jerry's Run Trail branches off to the west from Ramsey's Draft Trail.

Ramsey's Draft Trail continues with intermittent sections of the woods road and several long regions of chaos resulting from the flood.

At 6.6 km (4.1 mi.) Ramsey's Draft branches into a Left Prong and a Right Prong. Up to this point part of the trail was an old road, but it becomes a foot trail here and follows the Right Prong.

A trail sign and a USGS benchmark giving the elevation as 889 m (2,914 ft.) are located on the west, at the end of the old road section.

Ramsey's Draft Trail now begins to climb noticeably. You are traveling through an area with very large hemlocks. This is virgin timber—a rarity in Virginia. The hemlock forest continues far up the trail, though not to the ridgeline. There are few campsites along this section of the trail because of the steepness of the terrain.

The trail now climbs more steeply through open woods with large trees. At 8.1 km (5 mi.) the trail turns 90 degrees to the west. Near this bend, you will cross an underground stream coming from the east. With some careful searching you may find a few rocky campsites here in a beautiful setting. Ahead are small mossy waterfalls along Ramsey's Draft.

You may occasionally encounter a large tree that has fallen across the path, unless a trail crew has been through recently. Climb over these obstructions rather than going around them. The latter practice often causes erosion.

At 9.5 km (5.9 mi.) is the junction with Tearjacket Trail, coming in from the northeast. Lots of skunk cabbage grow here in the summer.

About 200 m (656 ft.) below this trail junction, cross Ramsey's Draft for the last time. The stream here is very small, but it is the last water you can count on finding. A hundred meters west of the trail junction is a campsite near the spring that is the source of the Right Prong of Ramsey's Draft, but which may be dry in late summer.

Continuing west along the Ramsey's Draft Trail from this junction, you will come to the beginning of the Hardscrabble Knob Trail at 0.6 km (0.4 mi.) more (10.1 km; 6.3 mi.). From here Ramsey's Draft Trail descends slightly toward its junction with the Shenandoah Mountain trail at 11.3 km (7 mi.).

You now have left the large trees far behind you. The hike here leads through younger woods with some undergrowth, including beautiful azaleas and many suckers of the American chestnut, which grow 3 to 7 m (10 to 20 ft.) tall from the old rootstocks before being attacked by the blight.

You will arrive at the Shenandoah Mountain Trail in a clear wooded area with many large trees (11.3 km; 7 mi.). The junction is marked by a row of six spruce trees planted fairly close together. There is a spring near the junction of Shenandoah Mountain and Ramsey's Draft trails, a few meters down the west slope of the mountain.

HARDSCRABBLE KNOB TRAIL

Length: 0.6 kilometers (0.4 miles)
Direction of travel: South
Difficulty: Easy
Elevation: 1,232–1,306 meters (4,040–4,282 feet)
Difference in elevation: 74 meters (242 feet)
Markings: None
Trail # 440A

How to get there: The trail begins at 9.3 km (5.8 mi.) up the Ramsey's Draft Trail. The trailhead can also be reached by hiking 1.1 km (0.7 mi.) down the Ramsey's Draft Trail from its terminus at the Shenandoah Mountain Trail.

Trail description: There is a much-used campsite—no water—at the trailhead, and a sign pointing to Hardscrabble Knob. You may find water at a spring several hundred meters east of the trailhead, along the Ramsey's Draft Trail, but this supply is dependable only from late fall through spring.

Hardscrabble Knob Trail climbs slightly but steadily to the south toward Hardscrabble Knob, at an elevation of

1,306 m (4,282 ft.). The knob is the highest point along Ramsey's Draft.

In summer, the trail may be heavily overgrown with fern and other plants. At 0.6 km (0.4 mi.) you will reach an abandoned cabin on the left side of the trail near the knob. There are several campsites here, although no water is available.

Hardscrabble Knob Trail continues for 50 m past the cabin to the rock outcropping which is Hardscrabble Knob. Views are obscured by trees in the summer and aren't exactly stupendous in winter, either.

JERRY'S RUN TRAIL

Length: 3.2 kilometers (2 miles)
Direction of travel: West
Difficulty: Moderate
Elevation: 769–964 meters (2,520–3,160 feet)
Difference in elevation: 195 meters (640 feet)
Markings: None, but trail obvious
Trail # 441
How to get there: The trail begins 3.4 km (2.1 mi.) up the Ramsey's Draft Trail. The opposite end can be reached via the Shenandoah Mountain Trail.
Trail description: The trail climbs steadily to the west and toward the Shenandoah Mountain Trail 3.2 km (2 mi.) away.

The trail crosses Jerry's Run several times but, except during very high water, most crossings can be made on rocks or by jumping. For the first 0.8 km (0.5 mi.), there are several established campsites ready for use and complete with fire rings.

At 2.6 km (1.6 mi.) you will enter a grassy open area at the former site of Sexton Cabin. The concrete foundation and the fireplace are all that remain of the cabin.

Jerry's Run Trail crosses the stream just below the cabin site and steadily climbs until it reaches the crest of Shenandoah Mountain and the Shenandoah Mountain Trail at 3.2 km (2 mi.).

By the latter trail, the junction with the northern end of the Ramsey's Draft Trail is 8.2 km (5.1 mi.) and with Forest Development Road 95, 12.9 km (8 mi.) to the north. U.S. 250 is 4.3 km (2.7 mi.) distant to the south.

WILD OAK TRAIL

Length: 8.4 kilometers (5.2 miles)
Direction of travel: West and north
Difficulty: Moderate to strenuous
Elevation: 705–1,256 meters (2,312–4,120 feet)
Difference in elevation: 551 meters (1,808 feet)
Markings: White plastic diamonds
Trail # 716

The Wild Oak Trail forms a 41.2 km (25.6 mi.) loop, only part of which lies within the Ramsey's Draft area. Most sections were formerly called by different names, which still appear on many maps. The sections described here were previously called the Dividing Ridge and Springhouse Ridge trails.

How to get there: Approaching from Churchville, turn off U.S. 250 to the right onto County Road 715 immediately after passing the bridge over the Calfpasture River. Approached from the west, the turnoff is just before the bridge and to the left. After the pavement ends at 5.3 km (3.3 mi.) the road becomes Forest Development Road 96. You will reach the trailhead, where FDR 96 crosses the height-of-land, 6.8 km (4.2 mi.) after leaving U.S. 250. There is a small parking space for three or four cars on the left.

The opposite end of this trail can be reached by continuing along FDR 96 to the junction with FDR 95. Turn left on 95. You will reach Camp Todd, with numerous un-developed campsites, 14.8 km (9.2 mi.) from U.S. 250. Walk along the trail at the sign describing the camp's history. About 20 m south of a water pump—before you reach it—the trail starts to the left across a small ravine.

Trail description: A berm blocks vehicle access to the trail to the west. At first the walking is rather level. About 500 m from the parking lot the trail divides. The Wild Oak Trail is straight ahead; an old woods road wanders off to the right along the hillside and then down again.

Follow the Wild Oak Trail, with its occasional white plastic diamonds. Shortly the trail starts climbing very steeply along the crest of Dividing Ridge, with loose rocks and dirt making the footing treacherous at times.

At 3.4 km (2.1 mi.) you will reach a saddle, where there usually is a small stagnant pond with no inflow or outflow. The water *cannot* be drunk even after treatment with Halazone tablets or by boiling. This section is grassy and full of mosquitoes and flies in the summer. There are a few limited views. The Bald Ridge Trail starts to the south near the pond, following along the crest of Bald Ridge and eventually descending to the picnic area at Braley Pond (11.1 km; 6.9 mi.).

The Wild Oak Trail climbs steeply from the other side of the pond, then levels, turning north.

About 25 m after the summit of Big Bald Knob, which is a grassy clearing with no views, you will come to a short new path on your right leading to the edge of the ridge and a beautiful view over the valley. After this side path, the main trail then descends to the junction with Tearjacket Trail at 6 km (3.7 mi.). There is a wilderness registry box at the intersection. To the west, Ramsey's Draft Trail is 1.9 km (1.2 mi.) down the Tearjacket Trail. (The closest water is a pool and spring on the Ramsey's Draft Trail near that junction.) Hardscrabble Knob Trail (via the Ramsey's Draft Trail) is 2.6 km (1.6 mi.) away.

Turn right to continue on the Springhouse Ridge section of the Wild Oak Trail. At first the walking is almost level, then the trail descends more steeply with several switchbacks, reaching Camp Todd at 8.4 km (5.2 mi.). About 300 m before reaching Camp Todd a creekbed, usually dry, lies below the trail to the right (south).

TEARJACKET TRAIL

Length: 1.9 kilometers (1.2 miles)
Direction of travel: Generally west
Difficulty: Easy
Elevation: 1,113–1,195 meters (3,650–3,920 feet)
Difference in elevation: 82 meters (270 feet)
Markings: None, but trail easy to follow
Trail # 426
How to get there: The Tearjacket Trail begins 2.4 km (1.5 mi.) from Camp Todd on Wild Oak Trail. The other end can be reached via Ramsey's Draft Trail 1.8 km (1.1 mi.) from its junction with Shenandoah Mountain Trail.
Trail description: Starting at the Wild Oak Trail, the Tearjacket Trail leads through open woods, first descending very slightly and then climbing gently to its junction with Ramsey's Draft Trail. There are no views along the way.

The trail does not lead over Tearjacket Knob, nor does any side trail that we could find. And, in our experience so far, Tearjacket Trail has not lived up to its descriptive name.

At the junction of Tearjacket and Ramsey's Draft trails you will find a nice campsite with a spring close by.

From this point Hardscrabble Knob Trail begins 0.6 km (0.4 mi.) to the west; Shenandoah Mountain Trail is 1.8 km (1.1 mi.) west, and FDR 95, via Shenandoah Mountain Trail, is 6.4 km (4 mi.) distant. To the east and south, via Ramsey's

Draft Trail, it is 6.1 km (3.8 mi.) to the beginning of Jerry's Run Trail and 9.5 km (5.9 mi.) to the parking facilities near U.S. 250.

BALD RIDGE TRAIL

Length: 11.1 kilometers (6.9 miles)
Direction of travel: Generally north
Difficulty: Difficult
Elevation: 880–1,170 meters (2,000–3,900 feet)
Difference in elevation: 830 meters (1,900 feet)
Markings: Intermittent yellow plastic diamonds
Trail # 496
How to get there: Approaching from Churchville via U.S. 250, turn right onto County Road 715 immediately after crossing the Calfpasture River. After 0.6 km (0.4 mi.), turn left to the Braley Pond Picnic Area, where parking is available. Follow the trail around the right side of Braley Pond and cross a footbridge over the stream that feeds the pond. Immediately after crossing the footbridge, turn right onto a woods road. This is the start of the Bald Ridge Trail.
Trail description: The Bald Ridge Trail shows signs of recent maintenance work in some places, but in other areas it has faded to invisibility. Even where it has completely vanished, however, its general route along the ridge can usually be followed without much difficulty. Carrying a topographic map and compass will help keep you headed in the right direction at a few points where side ridges branch off to the east or west.

From its starting point just above Braley Pond, the trail ascends very gently as a woods road and passes through three grassy game clearings within the first 0.8 km (0.5 mi.). Beyond the third clearing the trail crosses a small stream, and after another 50 m it turns right off the woods road.

A sign marks this point, and two log steps are set into the bank of the road.

From here the trail follows on or near a ridge for about 0.8 km (0.5 mi.) and then climbs at a steady rate along the hillside. In some places along this ascent there are excellent views of the mountains and valleys to the south through the open woods.

At several points, especially just after crossing ravines, the trail traverses regions of rather soft soil on a steep hillside and is badly eroded and very faint. It is usually easy to pick up again as it enters more solid ground. As you approach the top of the ridge, however, you will encounter a longer section of vanished trail. Ribbons or other markers may or may not be present to mark the route. If lost, you can simply continue up the hillside until you gain the crest. The trail itself reaches the ridgetop at 4.6 km (2.9 mi.), shortly after its proposed junction with the route of a new trail, now under construction, from the Mountain House Picnic Area.

From this point on, the trail follows the crest to the north or northeast, going over or around several small knobs or peaks. The highest points, rising at most 100 m above the ridgeline, are called The Peak, The Pinnacle, and Gordons Peak—none with a view. The trail has been maintained principally by occasional usage, so that it is clear and well worn where its course is obvious (such as along the top of narrow ridges) but becomes obscure or vanishes altogether in places where the best route is ambiguous.

For the first kilometer after reaching the top of Bald Ridge, it is easiest to bypass the peaks on the right (east) side. The last, and largest, of these is The Peak, the summit of which is an uninspiring tangle of dense brush.

After passing The Peak, continue to the north along Bald Ridge, climbing over the tops of subsequent knobs and sometimes bypassing them on the left (west) side. The trail is faint in many places but not necessary anyway: The open forest that grows along the ridgetop makes walking without a trail easy and, in fact, delightful. The wilderness feeling experienced along this seldom-traveled ridge is as fine as any you can obtain within the Ramsey's Draft Wilderness.

After Gordons Peak the trail, here fortunately well maintained, passes through a thicket of mountain laurel and finally ends at a small stagnant pond and the junction with Wild Oak Trail. To the right (east) it is 3.4 km (2.1 mi.) to FDR 96. To the left you can follow Wild Oak Trail to the junction with Tearjacket Trail (2.6 km; 1.6 mi.) and down to Camp Todd and FDR 95 (2.4 km; 1.5 mi.). It is 1.9 km (1.2 mi.) along Tearjacket Trail to Ramsey's Draft Trail.

SINCLAIR HOLLOW TRAIL

Length: 2.9 kilometers (1.8 miles)
Direction of travel: Southeast
Difficulty: Moderate
Elevation: 760–990 meters (2,500–3,250 feet)
Difference in elevation: 230 meters (750 feet)
Markings: None
Trail # 447D
How to get there: Approaching from Churchville, turn off U.S. 250 to the right onto County Road 715 immediately after passing the bridge over the Calfpasture River. Approached from the west, the turnoff is just before the bridge and to the left. The pavement ends at 5.3 km (3.3 mi.), and the road becomes FDR 96. At the junction with FDR 95 turn left. After about 12.1 km (7.5 mi.) the road will fork (keep right) and start to descend steeply. After 1.6 km (1 mi.) down the hill, turn left on FDR 64. After snaking along the hillside for 9.8 km (6 mi.), you come to a gate, which is only open from mid-October to January 1. It is 0.8 km (0.5

mi.) to the start of the Sinclair Hollow Trail on the left. The trail is only marked by a sign depicting a hiking figure.

The other end of the trail can be reached via the Shenandoah Mountain Trail.

Trail description: The Sinclair Hollow Trail starts on the left as an old logging road. The trail first crosses a streambed, then two "tank traps" to keep out ATVs.

About 0.5 km (0.3 mi.) later you will pass a game pond on the left. At 1.2 km (0.7 mi.) you come to a small grassy clearing.

The woods are at first mostly hemlocks and pines, with hardwoods interspersed. Later the forest is mostly deciduous.

During the first half of the hike you will cross the creek twice more. After that there is no other source of water along the trail.

At 1.6 km (1 mi.) the old logging road becomes a foot trail and begins to ascend steeply up the side of a ridge. Near the top the climb becomes more moderate along the side of the ridge until you gain the crest of Shenandoah Mountain.

The Sinclair Hollow Trail meets the Shenandoah Mountain Trail in a grassy clearing in a saddle. No sign marks the junction; only a small metal sign proclaims the wilderness boundary. There is also a trail register.

4. Crawford Mountain Area

Crawford Mountain is part of Augusta County's Great North Mountain, which forms the western boundary of the Shenandoah Valley and the first ridges of the Alleghenies.

Crawford Mountain itself apparently has always been woodland with few, if any, pioneer settlers. There is evidence, however, of early clearing over an extensive tract on the higher slopes of McKittrick's Ridge, perhaps for grazing. The remainder of the mountain had been logged over at least once on a commercial scale before its acquisition by the U.S. Forest Service in 1921. Since then, the mountain has been largely left alone. Management is under the multiple-use designation, but timbering so far has been limited to two or three relatively small tracts, all at the periphery. Game management likewise has remained minimal, with two small clearings and no road access. A corridor for a Virginia Electric and Power Company power line cuts across the northwestern corner.

In all, the tract is remarkably wild and unspoiled. Crawford Mountain is a very rewarding place for a hike: The trails are almost all closed to motorized traffic, the woods are deep, and the solitude is impressive.

Crawford Mountain consists of a ridge and its outliers and considerable lower land. The lowlands are broken terrain with many small ravines, hillocks, and streambeds. The mountain proper tends to be on the dry side, with few active streams. Quite a few of the creeks shown on maps dry up in late summer.

Trees cover the entire mountain. They are mostly medium-sized hardwoods, with a few large specimens. There is little understory, giving a feeling of openness to the woods. You can find occasional large white pines and hemlocks along

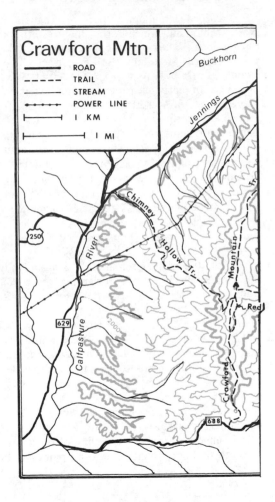

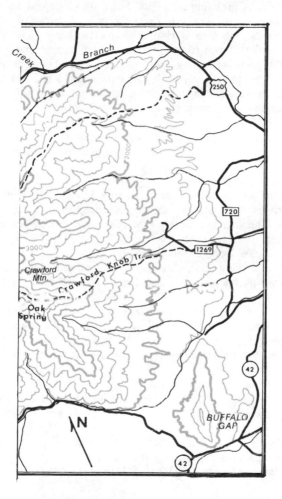

streams at lower elevations, where some rhododendrons also grow. There is probably no virgin forest on Crawford Mountain, although the aspect is certainly one of maturity. The best views can be seen during winter, after leaves have fallen, but a few unobstructed views may be had at any time from vantage points along the Crawford Mountain Trail.

In the spring, before the leaves come out, a wide variety of wildflowers, including dwarf iris, grow in the woods.

Especially for rock hounds: Some fossils, such as brachiopods, may be found in rocky streambeds and nearby cliffs or outcrops, particularly near County Road 688 west of the height-of-land between Crawford Mountain and Elliott Knob.

The climate of the region is generally mild, but in winter it is colder and snowier than in nearby Shenandoah Valley. Travelers in this season should be prepared for severe weather. The average winter temperature is 0 degrees Celsius (32 degrees Fahrenheit).

No camping or fire permits are necessary. The mountain is dry, and there is only one spring located close enough to trails to be useful (see map and Crawford Mountain description).

There are no private inholdings on Crawford Mountain. Some private land exists on the periphery of the tract.

There has been some abuse by ATVs on the Crawford Mountain Trail near Dunlap Hunter Access Road. The Forest Service has been talking about a possible rerouting of this portion of the trail.

In the Deerfield Ranger District, foot trails are marked by a yellow plastic diamond and ATV trails are marked in orange.

Maps: USGS Churchville, Elliot Knob, Stokesville, and West Augusta quadrangles, 7.5 minute series; Deerfield Ranger District map, George Washington National Forest.

CRAWFORD KNOB TRAIL

Length: 6.1 kilometers (3.8 miles)
Direction of travel: West
Difficulty: Moderate
Elevation: 554–1,137 meters (1,816–3,728 feet)
Difference in elevation: 583 meters (1,912 feet)
Markings Yellow plastic diamonds
Trail # 487

How to get there: Go 16.9 km (10.5 mi.) west from Staunton on U.S. 250 to the village of Lone Fountain. Turn left on County Road 720 and proceed 4.2 km (2.6 mi.) to a gravel road on the right, Forest Development Road 1269, with a sign reading SOUTH FORK MCKITTRICK'S ROAD. Drive in about 4.9 km (3 mi.); the Crawford Knob Trail leaves uphill to your left. Park there. (The road dead-ends just past this point.)

The opposite end of the trail can be reached via the Crawford Mountain Trail.

Trail description: At first the trail is an old woods road and passes through woods along a gently rising ridge. Ignore a side trail to the left near the trailhead.

At 1.8 km (1.1 mi.) the trail begins to climb steeply and continues to do so for 1 km (0.6 mi.). Then it passes through an extensive area of scrubby pine and laurel growth, permitting good views back over the Shenandoah Valley and, later, views southwest toward the southern main ridge of Crawford Mountain.

The trail in this section is overgrown and difficult to follow, which accounts for its absence from the USGS map. There are no trail markers in this section.

You will reach the wooded summit of Crawford Knob at 5 km (3.1 mi.). The knob is an outlier of the main Crawford Mountain ridge. You are 1,137 m (3,728 ft.) above sea level here.

The trail now descends slightly. You will arrive at the junction with the Crawford Mountain Trail at 6.1 km (3.8 mi.).

CRAWFORD MOUNTAIN TRAIL

Length: 12.5 kilometers (7.8 miles)
Direction of travel: Southwest
Difficulty: Moderate
Elevation: 543–1,150–818 meters (1,780–3,770–2,681 feet)
Difference in elevation: 607–332 meters (1,990–1,089 feet)
Markings: Yellow plastic diamonds
Trail # 443
How to get there: Take U.S. 250 west from Staunton. About 1.6 km (1 mi.) beyond the village of Lone Fountain, is Mack's Store. A sign on the right side of U.S. 250 indicates DUNLAP HUNTER ACCESS. Turn onto this access road immediately to the left of the store and go 1.5 km (0.9 mi.) to the end of the road. A sign marks the beginning of the trail.

To reach the opposite end, go through Buffalo Gap on Virginia Route 42 and turn right on County Road 688. Drive northwest for 6.1 km (3.8 mi.) to the trail on the north side of the road.

Trail description: For the first level 100 m the trail may be weedy, depending upon the season of the year.

After that the path becomes clearer, ascending more steeply along the side of a small ridge. After 200 m on this narrow trail, the path merges into an old woods road, which it then follows.

At 3.7 km (2.3 mi.) the trail starts climbing steeply up the mountain and finally gains the main ridge of Crawford Mountain.

Occasionally other old woods roads intersect with Crawford Mountain Trail—avoid them and follow the main trail. The path climbs gradually, with a few minor descents, through mature woods to the high point of the ridge (1,150 m; 3,770 ft.) at 3.9 km (2.4 mi.). What little view there is, mostly through woods, is best during the cold season after the leaves have fallen.

After this high point, the trail drops to slab the ridge on the left. At 8.8 km (5.5 mi.) the Crawford Knob Trail joins the Crawford Mountain Trail on the left. The junction is well marked.

Shortly thereafter, at 9 km (5.6 mi.), an unmarked trail branches off to the left and downhill. Descending 0.3 km (0.2 mi.), you will find Red Oak Spring.

Following the main trail from the spot where you left it to visit Red Oak Spring, you will quickly come upon the—again unmarked—terminus of the Chimney Hollow Trail on your right.

The Crawford Mountain Trail descends steeply at 9.3 km (5.8 mi.) for a short stretch, then levels out, still following the ridgeline. There are some very good views along this section.

The Crawford Mountain Trail continues to descend to the saddle between Crawford Mountain and its southern neighbor, Elliott Knob. (The saddle is called Dry Branch Gap on the USGS map.) At 12.5 km (7.8 mi.) you will reach County Road 688.

If you wish to hike the trail in the opposite direction, watch out for two trail junctions: At 2.7 km (1.7 mi.) the Red Oak Spring Trail branches off to the right, and at 11.4 km (7.1 mi.) a spur trail leading to private property branches off to the left.

CHIMNEY HOLLOW TRAIL

Length: 5.8 kilometers (3.6 miles)
Direction of travel: South
Difficulty: Moderate
Elevation: 590–1,113 meters (1,935–3,650 feet)
Difference in elevation: 523 meters (1,715 feet)
Markings: Yellow plastic diamonds
Trail # 487

How to get there: Go 29.6 km (18.4 mi.) west from Staunton on U.S. 250. Watch for the trail sign a few hundred meters after the highway reaches a height-of-land marked NORTH MOUNTAIN. Park along the side of the road. The trail leaves on the south side.

You can reach the other end of the trail from the Crawford Mountain Trail.

Trail description: At first the trail ascends gradually through the beautiful ravine of Chimney Hollow. Large hemlocks, white pines, and rhododendrons grow in this narrow valley, setting it apart from the area's usual oak woods.

After 2.3 km (1.4 mi.) you will reach the head of the ravine. There are a number of beautiful views all along this trail.

The trail now turns aside to skirt Coalpit Knob, a prominent outlier of the main Crawford Mountain ridge (elevation: 867 m; 2,841 ft.). If you wish to ascend the knob, you will have to bushwhack.

After rounding Coalpit Knob, the trail follows the connecting ridge. Oaks dominate the vegetation along this section of the trail.

At length the trail climbs the main Crawford Mountain ridge with one switchback to the left—avoid the faint trail to the right. Atop the ridge the Chimney Hollow Trail ends, after 5.8 km (3.6 mi.), at the Crawford Mountain Trail.

5. Elliott Knob Area

Elliott Knob, at 1,361 meters (4,463 feet), is the highest elevation in the George Washington National Forest. Like its neighbor to the immediate north, Crawford Mountain, Elliott Knob is located in Augusta County.

Elliott Knob consists of a mountain ridge and its outliers and considerable lower land, especially on the northwest side. On the ridge is a peak with the highest elevation in the forest: This, strictly speaking, is Elliott Knob. The rest of the ridge is Great North Mountain. Common usage, though, refers to the entire ridge as Elliott Knob, and we do likewise.

Few, if any, settlers appeared in the early history of Elliott Knob. Most of the area seems always to have been forest, although some evidence indicates clearing on the upper east face of the mountain before U.S. Forest Service acquisition. These places, which originally may have been highland pastures, have not recovered well. The mountain's west side shows considerable evidence of clearcutting at the lower levels, where there is also an extensive network of interconnected game clearings.

Forest Service plans call for continued timber harvest by clearcutting. A timber sale was scheduled for 1989/1990 off the Falls Hollow Trail. The logging road is scheduled to be closed after the operation is complete. A small parking area for hikers will be constructed off Virginia Route 42.

A fire tower is located atop the peak. An access road, which is closed to vehicles, leads to it from the east. Just below the mountain's summit on the east side is a large and unsightly UHF television transmission tower.

This mountain is generally higher, steeper, and more spectacular than Crawford Mountain. Despite the insults visited upon it, it remains a splendid peak. The entire west

101

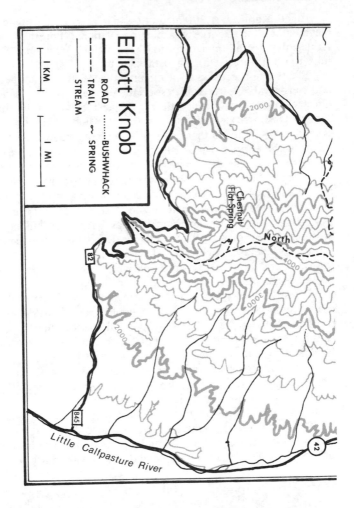

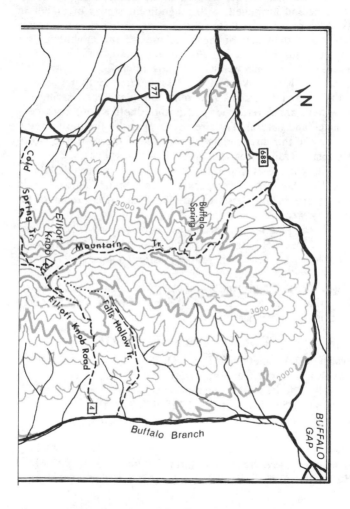

side of the main ridge, as well as its outliers, is particularly scenic and unspoiled, with magnificent stands of timber in its steep coves. The flora of these coves has a more northerly aspect than that of the remainder of the mountain. But botanical surprises can be found anywhere, and many high places on the upper flanks are only imperfectly known.

Elliott Knob, like Crawford Mountain, tends to be dry, with few active streams and only four developed springs.

There are several viewpoints on Elliott Knob, both constructed and natural. The fire tower provides the most sweeping view of the surrounding countryside. Otherwise, the North Mountain Trail offers the most scenic possibilities.

The climate is generally mild, similar to the climate of Crawford Mountain. Temperatures in summer as well as in winter are below those of the lowlands. Be prepared for freezing weather in winter.

No camping or fire permits are necessary on Elliott Knob.

The Deerfield Ranger District has marked foot trails in nonwilderness areas with yellow plastic diamonds; ATV trails are marked in orange.

Maps: USGS Elliott Knob and Augusta Springs quadrangles, 7.5 minute series; Deerfield Ranger District map, George Washington National Forest.

ELLIOTT KNOB ROAD

Length: 4.7 kilometers (2.9 miles)
Direction of travel: Generally west
Difficulty: Moderate to strenuous
Elevation: 648–1,361 meters (2,125–4,463 feet)
Difference in elevation: 713 meters (2,338 feet)
Markings: None needed
Trail # 444
How to get there: The trail starts 5.3 km (3.3 mi.) south of Buffalo Gap on Virginia Route 42. After a long level stretch,

the highway goes up a slight rise, near the top of which a gravel road will be seen branching off right and upward. This is Forest Development Road 4, and the numeral is marked on a low post at the intersection. Turning in there, you will immediately come upon a sign for Elliott Knob Trail, with the information that the trail is closed except to hikers and vehicles 61 cm (24 in.) wide or less. (Hikers beware!) There is room to park.

This road offers direct access to the summit of Elliott Knob from the east.

Trail description: The trail is actually a broad gravel road that takes a straightforward ridgetop route all the way to the summit and is something of a long pull in sunny, hot weather. It passes almost from beginning to end through tracts of head-high scrub of pine, oak, and laurel, indicative of past clearing. This makes for good views back over the Shenandoah Valley and, unfortunately, for a prostrating absence of shade. The road itself has somewhat treacherous footing, so watch your step carefully.

On the right, after 3.9 km (2.4 mi.), are two springs and a somewhat disreputable-looking pond.

At 4.7 km (2.9 mi.) you will reach the partly cleared summit (1,361 m; 4,463 ft.), with its fringe of planted spruce and larch and its fire tower, offering unobstructed views all around. This is the highest point in George Washington National Forest.

FALLS HOLLOW TRAIL

Length: 3.7 kilometers (2.3 miles); add 1.4 km (0.9 mi.) for bushwhack to North Mountain Trail
Direction of travel: Generally west
Difficulty: Strenuous
Elevation: 612–1,281 meters (2,008–4,200 feet)
Difference in elevation: 669 meters (2,192 feet)
Markings: Yellow plastic diamonds
Trail # 657

How to get there: Drive 4.8 km (3 mi.) south of Buffalo Gap on Virginia Route 42. The trail is an ungated woods road on the right. Just past it are the ruins of an old brick house, and a bit farther on is the beginning of Elliott Knob Road. Park alongside Route 42 until a scheduled timber sale is complete and the Forest Service has constructed a small parking area.

Upon entering the trail, you are confronted with a three-way intersection. Follow the yellow markers of the center path (gradual ascent), which is really a woods road. Unfortunately, there is traffic on it from four-wheel-drive vehicles—whose owners seem intent only on pushing their cars to the limit.

Trail description: The trail passes through a very beautiful mountain hollow, where mature hemlock, linden, and birch tower above the falls and pools of a charming brook.

Passing at first over low ridges, the trail threads an extensive area of game clearings, affording some views of the higher ridges ahead. A timber sale was scheduled close to Falls Hollow Trail for 1989/1990, and the scars are likely to remain visible for a few years.

At 2.4 km (1.5 mi.) the path picks up the little brook for the first time and proceeds uphill through an increasingly narrow gorge, never far from the stream. The forest scenery is very impressive.

The trail crosses the brook twice. At 3.7 km (2.3 mi.) the trail crosses the creek a third time and then begins to disintegrate rapidly.

From here on, the location of the trail is often doubtful. It is in turn overgrown, clogged by down timber, lost in the creek, and reduced to a treacherous boulder-strewn gully. Nonetheless, there are many whose hardihood and strong ankles will tempt them to press on. Forest Service maps show the trail turning left out of the hollow and connecting with Elliott Knob Road. At present, this turn is impossible to locate and will have to wait for a trail maintenance crew to be of any value to hikers.

In any case, after 1.4 km (0.9 mi.) more of scrambling up the hollow, you should arrive at the North Mountain Trail near the summit. Watch carefully for the narrow footpath. The Falls Hollow Trail ends here.

A left turn onto the North Mountain Trail will take you to the Elliott Knob Road. Turn right onto the road and in 0.5 km (0.3 mi.) you will reach the summit and lookout tower.

NORTH MOUNTAIN TRAIL

Length: 14.2 kilometers (8.8 miles)
Direction of travel: Generally southwest
Difficulty: Moderate
Elevation: 818–1,300–970 meters (2,681–4,263–3,182 feet)
Difference in elevation: 482–330 meters (1,582–1,081 feet)
Markings: Yellow plastic diamonds
Trail # 443
How to get there: Just south of Buffalo Gap on Virginia Route 42, turn right onto County Road 688, which is at first paved, then gravel, and proceed 6.1 km (3.8 mi.) to the height-of-

land between Elliott Knob and Crawford Mountain. Parking can be found on the south side of the road. The gated North Mountain Trail goes south and uphill from the parking area. This trail is a southern continuation of the Crawford Mountain Trail. The trail here is also called Elliott Knob Trail on some maps.

To get to the other end of the trail, follow Route 42 until 12.9 km (8 mi.) south of Buffalo Gap. Just past the village of Augusta Springs, you can see Forest Development Road 845 (gravel) on the right, with a post marking the road number. This road later turns into FDR 82. It is 7.2 km (4.5 mi.) to the height-of-land, whence the gated North Mountain Trail goes steeply uphill to the right.

Trail description: Leaving the parking area, the North Mountain Trail ascends what is really an extended ridge side of Elliott Knob. At 0.3 km (0.2 mi.) from the parking area, the trail drops from the ridge to the right to avoid posted private property. This well-graded detour regains the ridge at 1.3 km (0.8 mi.). Thence the trail climbs in step wise fashion through pleasant woods.

Reaching steeper slopes at 2.4 km (1.5 mi.), the trail turns aside from its ridge to climb across and around the buttress ridges of the mountain's upper flank, never very steeply. Including the original ridge, four such buttresses are rounded. Their dry southwestern sides are sparsely vegetated, offering both plentiful blueberries in season and many grand views up to the summit ridge and down southwest over spectacular terrain to the Deerfield Valley, with Shenandoah Mountain beyond. In the coves you will see magnificent forest growth.

On rounding the second ridge at 3.4 km (2.1 mi.), you will see an unmarked trail branching off to the right and downhill. This trail descends 0.3 km (0.2 mi.) to Buffalo Spring. Another trail branches off to the right 300 m after the trail to Buffalo Spring. It peters out shortly, so stay to the left.

At 4.8 km (3 mi.) the main trail attains the summit ridge and continues along it through woods for 0.3 km (0.2 mi.), before dropping off slightly to the left to round a minor peak.

Leaving the trail here and bushwhacking straight ahead a short distance to the top of the peak will reveal a large rock outcrop on the peak's west side, which affords superb views.

Shortly after regaining the ridgetop, the North Mountain Trail again slabs left to join the Elliott Knob Road at 7.6 km (4.7 mi.), 0.6 km (0.4 mi.) below the summit. Springs can be found a short distance left and down the road.

Turning right onto the road and following it up 0.3 km (0.2 mi.), you will find a trail with yellow markers turning off to the left. Take this trail to continue southwest along the summit ridge. (Elliott Knob Road goes on to the right and upward to the peak, where you can obtain excellent views of the surrounding countryside from the fire tower.)

At 0.2 km (0.1 mi.) past the junction, the Cold Spring Trail branches off to the right. A sign will mark the location for you.

About 0.5 km (0.3 mi.) farther on, the trail climbs out of the woods onto the so-called "Hogback," a secondary summit of the mountain (1,356 m; 4,447 ft.)—cleared during World War II as a potential navy radar site and now for the most part overgrown with scrub. Some views are afforded by scattered rockslides. Here, also, the trail widens to a rough jeep road.

Reentering the woods, the road descends gradually along the ridge. At 11.3 km (7 mi.) from the trailhead a side trail leaves on the right, which leads to the Chestnut Flat Spring, after an easy walk of 0.5 km (0.3 mi.).

At 14.2 km (8.8 mi.) the road ends at FDR 82—Hite Hollow Road—in a slight gap (970 m; 3,182 ft.).

If you hike the trail in the opposite direction, watch for the left turn of the North Mountain Trail off the Elliott Knob Road just above a power line pole. A post with yellow markers indicates the location of the trailhead, which is rather overgrown here.

COLD SPRING TRAIL

Length: 3.9 kilometers (2.4 miles)
Direction of travel: Generally east
Difficulty: Moderate to strenuous
Elevation: 729–1,312 meters (2,390–4,300 feet)
Difference in elevation: 583 meters (1,910 feet)
Markings: Yellow plastic diamonds
Trail # 445
How to get there: Go south of Buffalo Gap on Virginia Route 42 and turn right onto County Road 688, which is at first paved, then gravel. Go about 9.3 km (5.8 mi.)—3.2 km (2 mi.) past the height-of-land between Crawford Mountain and Elliott Knob and the start of the North Mountain Trail—to the junction with a good gravel road, Forest Development Road 77, on the left. The signs read TO HITE HOLLOW ROAD. Turn here. Make sure you do not take a road branching to the right from FDR 77 at 4.7 km (2.9 mi.). At 5.6 km (3.5 mi.) you will see a woods road on the left, accompanied by a sign on the right, with lettering on the reverse side only reading ELLIOT KNOB TRAIL: ELLIOT KNOB L. O. 3.2 KM (2 MI.). The woods road is passable by car for several hundred meters but is then reduced to a footpath. Park your car.

This trail offers access to the summit of Elliott Knob from the west.
Trail description: The trail almost immediately crosses a small brook, Still Run, and then follows it on the right. Sixty to

seventy paces after the crossing, depending upon your length of step, the trail rather obscurely turns right and away from the brook.

In another few meters the trail encounters an old woods road and ends. Turn left and look for yellow markers. The road is quite overgrown. A spruce grove will be on the right side of the road, and just past it there are superb blackberries in early August.

The so-called "Cold Spring" lies about 50 m south of the path, on a short but unmarked and overgrown side trail. We did not succeed in locating it. Nevertheless, other hikers claim it is easily found and is a source of water.

Soon the road narrows into a good graded trail and ascends via one of the mountain's many subsidiary ridges through pleasant woods. It then slabs across two adjoining ridges and makes an ascending traverse of the mountain's upper flank. The trail here passes through beautiful yellow birch woods and becomes considerably overgrown in summer.

The trail gains the summit ridge at 3.9 km (2.4 mi.) and ends at the North Mountain Trail. A sign marks the trailhead.

From here, turn left to reach the gravel Elliott Knob Road in 0.2 km (0.1 mi.), which in turn leads left to the summit in another 0.3 km (0.2 mi.).

Jefferson National Forest

6. James River Face Wilderness

The James River Face Wilderness consists of 35.6 square kilometers (8,800 acres) along the south bank of the James River, where the river breaks through the Blue Ridge Mountains. It is named for the cliffs and bluffs carved out of the 250 million-year-old Appalachian Mountains by the river. The James River Watergap is an excellent example of a geologic anticline. The area is composed of Precambrian and Paleozoic rock formations. Extensive uplifting and folding occurred in the formation of this section of the Blue Ridge Range.

The U.S. Forest Service administers this designated wilderness, whose most prominent features are its ruggedness and its inaccessibility. All trails climb sharply during their ascent toward the central ridges. These steep grades make hiking strenuous. And only an occasional rumbling of a Norfolk and Western Railroad coal train, along the north bank of the James, disturbs the stillness.

Probably few, if any, settlers ever tried making a living in this region, because of its unfriendly topography. At the beginning of this century the land adjacent to the James River was logged. Nevertheless, little evidence of this cutting is visible today, and the old logging roads have become hiking trails. During the 1960s some commercial timbering took place, but evidence of that is hard to find.

Scars of mining operations, however, are slow to heal, and two remain visible: one along the north bank of the river near Little Rocky Row, the second within the designated wilderness itself, along Petites Gap Road. Activities at the latter site terminated long before the area was designated a wilderness.

Two hydroelectric dams have been located on the James River. The dam at Balcony Falls was demolished in 1974 because it was no longer needed. The second, Snowden Dam, is situated just above the point where U.S. 501 crosses the river.

Old jeep trails in the James River Face Wilderness are no longer open to motorized vehicles. Certain designated paths may be opened to horses, but it would be wise to check with the local ranger before taking any animals there.

Chestnut oak, pitch pine, Virginia pine, table-mountain pine, yellow poplar, red and white oak, and hickory predominate in the woods. In certain places mountain laurel grows thickly. Among the Belfast and Gunter Ridge trails, particularly, galax covers the ground.

The Appalachian Trail (AT) is the most-hiked trail in the tract, and the immediate surroundings of its one shelter show very heavy use. Avoid taking large groups into the Face, especially overnight, because flat camping sites are rare. Staying at the AT shelter may be a crowded affair if other hikers are using it the same night.

Car camping on the perimeter of the area is another alternative and likely to be more pleasant than staying at the often overcrowded shelter. The land at the perimeter is rather flat, and many camping spots are available.

Try to plan your trip in the off-season rather than at a time when everybody goes hiking. You will enjoy your stay more if you do not encounter a steady stream of people along the trails. If you go during the winter, take warm clothes. It is cold in the Face and, if the wind is blowing too, it can be numbing! During the summer, long pants can be an advantage, as some trails wander through brier patches, nettles, and poison ivy.

Water is scarce on the ridges of which the Face largely consists.

When visiting the Face for one or two days, cars can be parked along the sides of roads, or in indentations in the

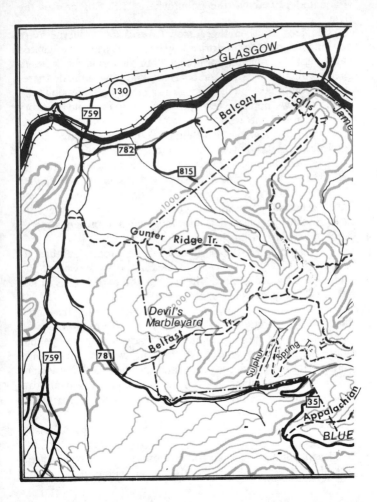

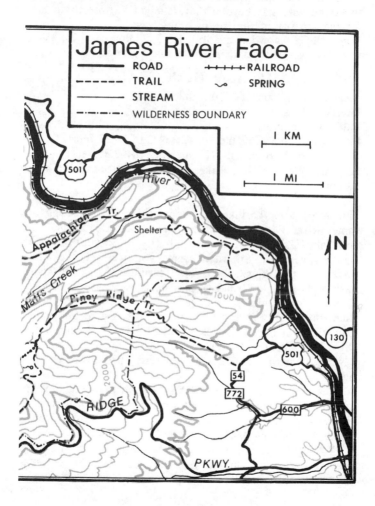

forest at trailheads, without too much worry. But if you plan to extend your stay beyond that, it might be wise to arrange for the security of the car in other ways.

Maps: USGS Snowden quadrangle, 7.5 minute series; Glenwood Ranger District map, Jefferson National Forest.

APPALACHIAN TRAIL

Length: 16.9 kilometers (10.5 miles)
Direction of travel: North and east
Difficulty: Strenuous
Elevation: 722–937–219 meters (2,369–3,073–720 feet)
Difference in elevation: 215–718 meters (704–2,353 feet)
Markings: White blazes. Take care to follow blazes at intersections.
Trail # 1
How to get there: To hike the Appalachian Trail through the James River Face, you will need a car shuttle. From Glasgow take U.S. 501 southeast. Shortly after you cross the James River near Snowden Dam, you will see the white blazes for the Appalachian Trail turning off to the right. Park one car off the road to pick up at the end of the hike. Continue on in the second car on U.S. 501 south to the Blue Ridge Parkway and turn south on it. Go to the Petites Gap exit and Forest Development Road 35 (County Road 781). You will see the AT's white blazes almost immediately. Park your car off the road and start up the trail on your right.
Trail description: Starting at Petites Gap on FDR 35, the Appalachian Trail climbs, at times very steeply, until it reaches Highcock Knob (937 m; 3,073 ft.). The trail leads through woods without any particularly good views along this stretch.

We highly recommend long pants and maybe even a long-sleeved shirt when hiking this part of the trail in summer—waist-high nettles and poison ivy will keep your attention until a little past the top on the other side of High-cock Knob.

The descent is at first very steep and then continues more moderately downhill via a long switchback.

At 3.8 km (2.4 mi.) there is a spring about 120 m from the trail.

Continuing 0.8 km (0.5 mi.) along the AT through pleasant woods, you will come upon the Sulphur Spring Trail. To your left the Sulphur Spring Trail goes downhill until it meets County Road 78l (FDR 35). The Piney Ridge Trail branches right from the AT a few paces up the hill. You may encounter stretches of an old fire road that used to come up the Sulphur Spring Trail and continue along the ridge to Balcony Falls Trail. Be careful to follow the white blazes of the Appalachian Trail.

The AT sometimes bypasses peaks and follows steep hillsides, and in other places it travels over saddles and long ridges.

After 0.8 km (0.5 mi.) the trail veers off to the left at almost a right angle. The AT follows a steep hillside, where no good views through the thick deciduous woods are available.

At 6.9 km (4.3 mi.) the AT arrives at the end of the Belfast Trail, on the left.

The AT then descends on the other side of the hill, crossing the old road again. At this point the Balcony Falls Trail runs off to the left.

Follow the white blazes. Now the AT steeply descends the mountainside in a series of switchbacks. The view of the rapids of the James River, Snowden Dam below them, and the bluffs dropping vertically down to the water are spectacular. You have the best vantage point at the northern end of each switchback. Mountain laurel and rhododendrons are abundant along the trail.

At the base of the switchbacks you will find a little stream with water.

At 4 km (2.5 mi.) farther down the trail—continuing to descend steeply—you will reach Matts Creek Shelter. There are several good campsites around the shelter, but the area shows signs of heavy use. A creek flows close by.

Passing the shelter, the AT ascends, in part steeply, the side of a mountain. It skirts a ridge, providing some good views of the James River, then drops and soon levels off briefly. The final descent to U.S. 501, of approximately 1.3 km (0.8 mi.), is steep in places. The total distance from the Matts Creek Shelter to 501 is 4 km (2.5 mi.).

PINEY RIDGE TRAIL

Length: 5.6 kilometers (3.5 miles)
Direction of travel: West
Difficulty: Moderate to strenuous
Elevation: 280–756 meters (920–2,480 feet)
Difference in elevation: 476 meters (1,560 feet)
Markings: Blue blazes; trail infrequently used and somewhat obscure at times
Trail # 2
How to get there: From Glasgow take U.S. 501 southeast across the James River. Turn right on FDR 54 2.3 km (1.4 mi.) after crossing the river. The trail starts 1 km (0.6 mi.) from U.S. 501. A trail sign marks the beginning.

You can reach the other end of the trail via the AT.
Trail description: At first the trail is an old logging road leading through woods and closed to motorized vehicles.

After climbing over a high berm, take the right-hand fork of the road. It climbs moderately for a short stretch and then, with a left turn, continues almost level.

During times of high water you may encounter a muddy wildlife pond. Shortly you will arrive at a fork.

Keep to the left, along the ridgetop. The trail now turns into an old woods road, with trees on both sides, and is pleasant to walk. The rate of the climb increases somewhat.

After a short stretch through pine woods, the road ends and the foot trail begins. It makes the first of several switchbacks and starts a steep climb. The trail is very narrow in places as it threads its way along the side of a steep slope. In these lower switchbacks the trail is rather obscure, so watch carefully.

The hike leads you now through deciduous woods. You are facing into a narrow ravine. Shortly before reaching the end of the ravine, the trail switches back on itself. Continue along the trail—there are two more switchbacks. The trail is still faint, but becomes quite distinct higher up. A sign marks the boundary of the wilderness area.

After the final turn, you will find yourself walking through pines again along a hillside. Reaching a saddle, the trail ascends more steeply along a ridge. It then runs almost horizontally along a steep hillside.

Shortly thereafter you will come to more pine woods and a junction with an old woods road. Go straight ahead here. (The right fork is overgrown and leads nowhere.)

The hike through woods of pine, hemlock, and laurel along this section of the trail is very pleasant. The trees are beginning to reclaim the road and convert it into a footpath.

The trail climbs at a moderate rate straight up the ridge. It ends at the AT at 5.6 km (3.5 mi.), just past a group of young pines growing in the middle of the old road. A signpost marks the trail junction.

BELFAST TRAIL

Length: 4.5 kilometers (2.8 miles)
Direction of travel: East
Difficulty: Moderate to strenuous

Elevation: 305–808 meters (1,000–2,650 feet)
Difference in elevation: 503 meters (1,650 feet)
Markings: Intermittent blue blazes; trail generally easy to follow
Trail # 9
How to get there: From Glasgow take Virginia Route 130 west to County Road 759. Go left on 759, crossing the James River, and drive 5 km (3.1 mi.) to County Road 781. Go left on 781 for 1.9 km (1.2 mi.) to the trail, on the left-hand side of the road. The trailhead is marked by a sign.

You can reach the other end of the trail via the Appalachian Trail.

Trail description: The Belfast Trail starts with a bridge across the East Fork of Elk Creek. At the far end of the bridge you will find a sign telling you the closest trail junctions—3.9 km (2.4 mi.) to the Gunter Ridge Trail and 4.5 km (2.8 mi.) to the Appalachian Trail. A few steps more and you will pass stone pillars announcing Camp Powhatan. This, apparently, was a summer camp. At any rate, it has not been used for quite some time.

Stay on the main trail, leaving side trails that invite exploration for another day. Shortly you will pass large concrete foundations, but any indications of what the buildings may have been have long since disappeared. A crossing of Belfast Creek is just ahead; it can be hopped across nicely on rocks.

The trail forks several times. Watch out for signs and blazes, and stay on the section that ascends gently but steadily. There is a possible campsite near a fork in the road. The right-hand branch of the trail crosses a stream with water, but on the other side it is overgrown and unused. Take the left-hand fork.

For a while there are many pines along the trail. The trail climbs gently but steadily, then levels off for a short stretch. It crosses the creek and immediately crosses back again. The stream can be hopped over on stones.

The trail now begins to climb more steeply, passing through mostly deciduous woods. The higher you climb, the steeper the trail gets.

At about the halfway point of the trail, you will arrive at Devil's Marbleyard, a big rockslide. At the lower end of the slide you will pass, on your right, a pretty waterfall down a vertical rock wall. When we hiked the trail in midwinter, the fall was frozen into many big icicles and looked spectacular. In times of drought this waterfall too may dry up.

Climbing very steeply, the trail skirts the foot of the rockslide. An obscure little path branches off to the left, leading to the slide itself and a view, if you get to the top.

After this very steep stretch, the Belfast Trail returns to a more gradual climb alongside the stream. There are a few smaller rockslides to the left of the trail, but they are nothing much to speak of.

Bending to the left, the grade diminishes to gentle. The trail heads around to the top of a ravine, where there is a beautiful winter view of a deep valley. The trees roundabout are mostly deciduous and probably block the view when the leaves are out.

The trail gets a bit steeper and climbs to a saddle, where the Gunter Ridge Trail terminates on the left (3.9 km; 2.4 mi.).

The Belfast Trail turns right and continues to climb moderately for a short stretch. It then descends slightly to end at the Appalachian Trail at 4.5 km (2.8 mi.).

GUNTER RIDGE TRAIL

Length: 7.2 kilometers (4.5 miles)
Direction of travel: East
Difficulty: Moderate to strenuous

Elevation: 244–768 meters (800–2,517 feet)
Difference in elevation: 524 meters (1,717 feet)
Markings: Blue blazes
Trail # 8
How to get there: From Glasgow take Virginia Route 130 west to County Road 759. Go left for 2.4 km (1.5 mi.) on 759 to the trailhead, which is marked by a sign.

You can reach the other end of the trail via the Belfast Trail.

Trail description: Starting on the left side of County Road 759, the Gunter Ridge Trail first follows a dirt road. The road forks near a white house with green trim. Take the right fork. Follow it along a fence and take another right turn at the barn. The road continues along the fence. Now you will begin to see the blue blazes marking the trail.

A little farther along there is another fork in the road. This time, take the left branch. Cross a small stream. The road passes through a wooded area containing beech, hemlock, pine, dogwood, hickory, and oak trees.

The road divides again and the trail follows the right fork. Watch the blazes carefully.

Two more roads branch off, one to the right and one to the left. Follow the blue blazes.

Now hemlocks are getting sparse and mountain laurel takes their place. You will find some galax, with its shiny red and green leaves, along the trail.

You will come upon another fork in the road: Take the left branch. Shortly after this fork, the trail becomes passable only on foot. The stream that it follows for a while may only run part of the year.

After passing the junction where another trail comes from the left (follow the blazes), the Gunter Ridge Trail begins to climb noticeably, leaving the stream in the ravine below to the right. Switchbacks start shortly after this, some eighteen of them. Along the way, you will see a few good spots for viewing the valley below and your starting point, especially in winter. The trees roundabout are mostly deciduous.

The trail continues to climb up the ridge and passes over a knob. After a short dip, it follows the ridge. It then skirts the second ridgetop, leaving it to the left, and continues level to end at the Belfast Trail at 7.2 km (4.5 mi.).

BALCONY FALLS TRAIL

Length: 8 kilometers (5 miles)
Direction of travel: East and south
Difficulty: Moderate to strenuous
Elevation: 229–789 meters (750–2,588 feet)
Difference in elevation: 560 meters (1,838 feet)
Markings: Blue blazes
Trail # 7
How to get there: From Glasgow take Virginia Route 130 west to County Road 759. Go left on 759, crossing the James River, and then turn left on County Road 782. Go to the end of the road and park in the "Lochei Tract" parking lot. The trail starts at a sign a few meters up the road over the fence on the south side. Do not follow the track into the cow pasture.

The other end of the trail can be reached via the AT.
Trail description: The trail starts out as an old woods road through attractive pine and deciduous woods. With only minor ups and downs, the road continues for 2.4 km (1.5 mi.). Close to the place where it turns into a foot trail, you will find some streambeds with water, though they may dry up in late summer and fall. There is no other water along the trail. A sign indicates the wilderness boundary.

Shortly thereafter the trail begins to climb steeply via innumerable switchbacks. The vegetation consists largely of pines and laurel.

At the top of the switchbacks you can get a good view of the James River and its rapids (4 km; 2.5 mi.).

The trail now continues almost level along a narrow ridge for a stretch. A single switchback leads to a broader ridge. The trail climbs moderately up it through deciduous woods. Reaching the top, the trail turns right, bypassing some large rocks. It then descends for a short distance.

At 5.6 km (3.5 mi.) the trail turns into an old woods road. You will find a Forest Service sign here supplying various distances: Locher Tract 6.5 km (4 mi.), Appalachian Trail 2.4 km (1.5 mi.), Petites Gap Road 10.4 km (6.5 mi.).

The road ascends gently, for the most part, through very rocky pine woods. On your right you will see a stone slide in Sawmill Hollow. A deep ravine, also on your right, follows. Rocky pine woods continue on both sides of the trail.

After a sharp left turn immediately before the ridgetop, the Balcony Falls Trail ends at the Appalachian Trail. A sign at the trail junction furnishes distances to different points: Locher Tract 8 km (5 mi.), Matts Creek Shelter 4.5 km (2.8 mi.).

SULPHUR SPRING TRAIL

Length: 4.8 kilometers (3 miles)
Direction of travel: Generally east
Difficulty: Moderate
Elevation: 442–747 meters (1,450–2,450 feet)
Difference in elevation: 305 meters (1,000 feet)
Markings: None
Trail # 3001
How to get there: From Glasgow take U.S. 501 south to the Blue Ridge Parkway and turn south on it. Go to the Petites Gap exit and FDR 35 (County Road 781). Go past the white

blazes of the Appalachian Trail and continue uphill in some long switchbacks. Shortly afterward you will come to a small bridge across Sulphur Spring and the trailhead on the right. There are two boulders and a trail sign. Parking space is enough for two or three cars.

Trail description: The Sulphur Spring Trail starts as an old road with a stream on the right.

After about 50 m (160 ft.) you will encounter a trail register indicating that this is a "foot and horse trail." Two thirds of the way up, though, this trail becomes too narrow and overgrown for horses.

The trail leaves the creek after 200 m (600 ft.), passing a sign on the left indicating SULPHUR SPRING. The spring, which is just off the trail, had some standing water in it in mid-winter.

Eventually the trail rejoins the stream and then crosses it. The creek, only one or two meters wide, can be easily negotiated.

The trail now starts to climb more noticeably. There are some nice views of Thunder Ridge to the south and of the length of Petites Gap. We hiked the trail in winter, but some of the views may still be there when the leaves are out.

Some maintenance has been done, but the brush eventually becomes waist high in places. This poses no problem to the hiker. The trail continues to ascend, hugging the side of the ridge. You can duck under the many small pines growing in and along the trail.

After a while you will come to an inconspicuous rock wall on your left. It is about 6 m (15 to 20 ft.) high. If you climb up, you will be rewarded with a great view.

Soon afterward you will reach the junction with the Appalachian Trail. Going north from here it is 8.2 km (5.1 mi.) to Matts Creek Shelter, 12.4 km (7.7 mi.) to Snowden Bridge. To the south it is about 0.8 km (0.5 mi.) to Marble Springs and 4.3 km (2.7 mi.) to Petites Gap along the AT.

7. Mountain Lake Wilderness

The Mountain Lake area is a high massif situated northwest of the town of Blacksburg in Virginia's Giles and Craig counties and West Virginia's Monroe County. The Mountain Lake Wilderness measures 43.5 square kilometers (10,700 acres).

Before the U.S. Forest Service acquired the land in the early part of this century, it had been largely cut over. As a result, most of the stands in the forest are roughly of even age. The Forest Service has logged only a little more than 0.4 square kilometers (100 acres), and the forest is beginning to mature.

Mountain Lake is one of only two natural lakes in Virginia, the other being Lake Drummond in the Dismal Swamp near Norfolk. The lake was first noted by a survey party in 1751. At that time raiding parties of Indians still roamed Virginia. During the Civil War, the Salt Sulphur Turnpike—now County Roads 700 and 613—was used to transport troops and matériel across the mountain. When Union forces retreated in 1864, they discarded ammunition and other heavy items at a place now known as Minié Ball Hill. (Minié balls were bullets used in the nineteenth century.) You can also find arrowheads throughout the Mountain Lake area.

In 1960 the Forest Service created a 6.1 square kilometer (1,500 acre) scenic area comprising Wind Rock, Lone Pine Peak, War Spur Branch, with its virgin trees, and War Spur Overlook. The Mountain Lake Wilderness was established in 1984 and increased to a total size of 43.5 square kilometers (10,700 acres) in 1988.

There are three forest zones in the Mountain Lake region. The Canadian Zone—generally above 1,220 meters (4,000 feet)—has red spruce, hemlock, yellow birch, and many other

129

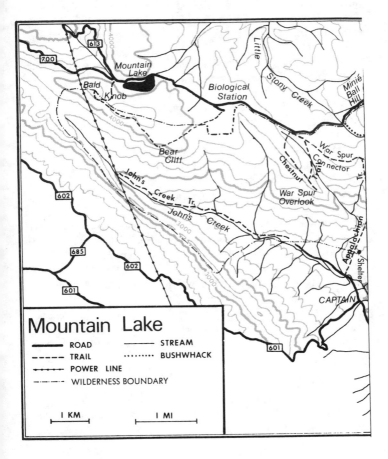

Mountain Lake

- ▬▬▬ ROAD
- - - - - TRAIL
- •••••• POWER LINE
- —••—••— WILDERNESS BOUNDARY
- ——— STREAM
- ········ BUSHWHACK

| 1 KM | 1 MI |

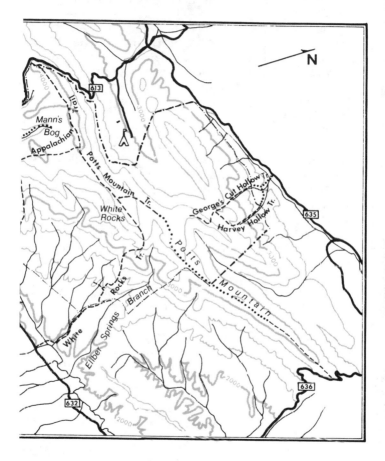

trees which are found mostly on high southern peaks. The forest around the edge of Mountain Lake itself reflects this zone, but the lake and its drainage basin are not part of the wilderness.

The Transition Zone—between 760 meters and 1,220 meters (2,500 feet and 4,000 feet)—predominates because most of the land lies in this altitude range. Various oaks, as well as hickories, walnuts, yellow poplars, Virginia and table-mountain pine, and other less frequent species occur throughout the Transition Zone. American chestnuts were once plentiful.

In the Upper Austral or Upper Carolinian Zone—generally 760 meters (2,500 feet) and below—grow various kinds of pine and oak, maples, eastern redbud, black walnuts, sassafras, locusts, cherries, and many more. You will find this vegetation mostly along John's Creek drainage. This zone shares much of the same flora with the Piedmont Zone of central Virginia.

More than nine hundred kinds of flowering plants have been identified in the scenic area alone. Rhododendrons are plentiful throughout the region, forming dense stands in several places. Mountain laurel and flame azaleas add charm and grace to the woods and make tough going for the bushwhacker. Greenbrier, raspberries, blackberries, and—at lower elevations—poison ivy are common. Many mushrooms and fungi, poisonous as well as edible, can be found. The height of the mushroom season is late July through August. Use extreme caution in identifying and eating mushrooms—in fact, abstain altogether unless you are a true expert in this field.

Timber rattlesnakes, copperheads, and black snakes (the last nonvenomous) are fairly common in the Mountain Lake area. Among the nine or ten species of salamander found, the red-backed salamander is the most prevalent. According to biologists at the University of Virginia's Mountain Lake Biological Station, more than one hundred species of birds have been recorded. You can find native brook trout in Little Stony Creek, John's Creek, War Branch, and White Rock Branch.

The eastern continental divide coincides with the ridgetops of Salt Pond Mountain, Potts Mountain, and John's Creek Mountain. Rain falling into the John's Creek drainage flows into the Atlantic Ocean, and water running into Little Stony Creek and White Rock Branch flows into the Gulf of Mexico.

At Bald Knob and Bear Cliff there are some outcrops of sandstone bedrock, deposited as sediment about 400 million years ago during the Silurian period. Outcrops at War Spur Overlook, Wind Rock, and White Rocks are probably of similar age and origin.

The climate is characterized by marked changes in weather. Annual precipitation exceeds 100 centimeters (40 inches). The temperature ranges from a record low of minus 32 degrees Celsius (minus 26 degrees Fahrenheit) to a maximum of approximately 29 degrees Celsius (85 degrees Fahrenheit). Summer thunderstorms are frequent, so go prepared with rain gear.

There are a number of good camping spots in the area, but water may be a problem at high elevations. If you plan to do any hiking along trails that are overgrown and hard to follow, take along topographic maps and a compass. That, of course, applies also to bushwhacking.

No camping or fire permits are necessary at this time.

Maps: USGS Interior, Waiteville, Eggleston, and Newport quadrangles, 7.5 minute series.

BIOLOGICAL-STATION-TO-BEAR-CLIFF TRAIL

Length: 1.4 kilometers (0.9 mile)
Direction of travel: South
Difficulty: Easy
Elevation: 1,165–1,250 meters (3,820–4,100 feet)
Difference in elevation: 85 meters (280 feet)
Markings: None; trail quite obvious
How to get there: Take U.S. 460 west from Blacksburg, past Newport, to the junction with County Road 700. Turn right and follow 700—or 613, as it is called beyond the Mountain Lake Hotel. Go past the hotel to the Mountain Lake Biological Station. This trail, as well as the trail system behind the Biological Station, is subject to private property rights and should not be used without permission. See the caretaker of the station.

The other end of the trail is reached via the Bear-Cliff-to-Bald-Knob Trail.

Trail description: At the entrance of the Biological Station grounds, the road forks. On your right will be a metal gate next to a tree with a NO TRESPASSING sign. Go through the gate and up the narrow road 0.8 km (0.5 mi.) to a small, wire-fenced springhouse. A foot trail continues on around the right side of the springhouse and gently winds uphill through mixed deciduous forest.

In a little while you will arrive at a short, steeper stretch, which takes you up to the broad ridge of Salt Pond Mountain.

Bear Cliff is located 0.5 km (0.3 mi.) across the crest, just past the point where the trail starts to descend the other side. It is a descending series of four or five sandstone tiers, each about 30 m (100 ft.) long, 6 to 12 m (20 to 40 ft.) high, and separated from each other by a space of 3 to 5 m (10 to 15 ft.). The highest rock face measures no more than 18 m (60 ft.), but there are some interesting boulder problems for rock climbers.

The views to the east and south are good. On a clear day you can see the Peaks of Otter, northeast of Roanoke, and parts of Blacksburg, Christiansburg, and Radford, Virginia.

BEAR-CLIFF-TO-BALD-KNOB TRAIL

Length:a 3.7 kilometers (2.3 miles)
Direction of travel: Southwest
Difficulty: Moderate
Elevation: 1,251–1,324 meters (4,100–4,340 feet)
Difference in elevation: 73 meters (240 feet)
Markings: None; trail may be difficult to follow. Carry map and compass.
How to get there: Via the Biological-Station-to-Bear-Cliff Trail, having received permission to hike it from the caretaker at the Biological Station.

To reach the other end of the trail, drive west from Blacksburg on U.S. 460, past Newport, until you arrive at the junction with County Road 700. Turn right and follow 700 to the Mountain Lake Hotel. Park there.

Hiking on this trail in either direction requires permission from the Mountain Lake Hotel caretaker because it is subject to private property rights.
Trail description: From the base of the highest tier at Bear Cliff, go southwest along the line of the cliff, gradually ascending a rocky gully. After 100 m, about where the cliff peters out, you should find a trail leading to the ridgetop of Salt Pond Mountain.

In 0.5 km (0.3 mi.) this trail goes through a typical southern thicket, with lots of mountain laurel. Brief glimpses of the Bald Knob microwave relay station are visible from some places in the thicket.

After you have passed the thicket, you will arrive at a marshy place with scattered hemlocks and some blazed trees. The trail may be hard to follow here; stay on the crest of the ridge and continue heading southwest.

At 2.1 km (1.3 mi.) from Bear Cliff you should meet a service road coming up Bald Knob from the Mountain Lake Hotel. Follow this road for 0.5 km (0.3 mi.) to the top of the mountain. Bald Knob is the highest point for many miles around, and the view is great.

You can walk back down the service road to the hotel and County Road 700.

CHESTNUT TRAIL–WAR SPUR OVERLOOK–WAR SPUR CONNECTOR TO APPALACHIAN TRAIL

Length: 4 kilometers (2.5 miles)
Direction of travel: Circuit
Difficulty: Easy
Elevation: 1,153–1,068 meters (3,780–3,500 feet)
Difference in elevation: 85 meters (280 feet)
Markings: Sign with trail diagram at trailhead; trail easy to follow
How to get there: From Blacksburg take U.S. 460 west, past the town of Newport, until the junction with County Road 700. Turn right and follow 700, or 613, as it is later numbered. Go past the Mountain Lake Hotel and the Mountain Lake Biological Station. About 2.6 km (1.6 mi.) later, look for a small parking lot on the right side of the road. The trail sign reads MOUNTAIN LAKE SCENIC AREA HIKING TRAILS. Park your car there.

This is a nice circuit hike with a pretty view.

Trail description: Go right (south) at the sign, crossing a small footbridge. The trail rises gently along War Spur to its rather broad crest.

The trail threads its way through mixed deciduous forest, past many fallen or leaning old chestnut trees, to the side trail to War Spur Overlook.

The overlook provides a good view of a stand of virgin trees along War Branch. Retrace your steps along the Overlook Trail to the point where you left the Chestnut Trail to continue the circuit.

Back on the main trail, you pass through a couple of switchbacks, then go downhill through a rhododendron archway to the virgin forest. There you will encounter War Branch and enjoy the beauty of the old majestic trees. The stream drains from an area of heavy human use.

Cross the stream and follow the Chestnut Trail out of War Branch Hollow. The trail now leads through teaberry country.

At 3.5 km (2.2 mi.) you will arrive at the War Spur Connector with the Appalachian Trail. If you turn left at this T-junction, you will be back at the parking lot in 0.5 km (0.3 mi.).

If you wish to go to the AT, turn right at the T-junction. For 1.6 km (1 mi.) you will walk along a wide grassy path. On the lower slopes to your right is a virgin stand of hemlocks. Then the path descends about 60 m (200 ft.) and joins the Appalachian Trail in a bend.

MANN'S BOG

Length: 1.1 kilometer (0.7 mile)
Direction of travel: Generally north
Difficulty: Easy to moderate
Elevation: 1,086–1,171 meters (3,560–3,840 feet)
Difference in elevation: 85 meters (280 feet)

Markings: None

How to get there: Take U.S. 460 west from Blacksburg, past the town of Newport, until the junction with County Road 700. Turn right and follow 700—or 613, as it is called after passing the Mountain Lake Hotel. Go past the hotel and the Mountain Lake Biological Station. Pass the trail sign reading MOUNTAIN LAKE SCENIC AREA HIKING TRAILS. Park on the right close to the point where 613 crosses Little Stony Creek, just beyond a small clearing.

This is a fairly easy bushwhacking hike. Carry map and compass, though.

Trail description: Leaving from the right side of the road, bushwhack up Little Stony Creek. The hike will take you up a gently sloping hollow through woods.

A little later the steepness increases slightly for about 100 m.

When you reach the top of the hollow, you will find yourself in a flat little valley. Here Little Stony Creek has its source in Mann's Bog.

Red spruce and hemlock grow in the bog, and its floor is covered with sphagnum moss. The moss is a delicate little plant and easily crushed. Walk barefoot on it to protect it and feel its soft springiness under your feet. No synthetic carpet can compare. (Besides, you'll keep your boots dry.)

Return to your car the way you came, along the creek.

APPALACHIAN TRAIL

Length: 7.2 kilometers (4.5 miles)
Direction of travel: Generally east and south
Difficulty: Moderate to strenuous
Elevation: 1,259–616 meters (4,128–2,020 feet)
Difference in elevation: 643 meters (2,108 feet)
Markings: White blazes
Trail # 1

How to get there: Take U.S. 460 west from Blacksburg, past Newport, until you arrive at the junction with County Road 700. Turn right and follow 700, or 613, as it is called after passing the Mountain Lake Hotel. Go past the Mountain Lake Hotel and the Mountain Lake Biological Station. Pass the trail sign reading MOUNTAIN LAKE SCENIC AREA HIKING TRAILS. Watch for the spot, about 6 km (3.7 mi.) later, where the Appalachian Trail crosses the road on the ridge of Potts Mountain just before the road starts a steep descent on the other side.

Trail description: The Appalachian Trail continues on the right side of the road on the ridge of Potts Mountain and goes gently uphill.

At 0.5 km (0.3 mi.) you will pass Wind Rock, which is located 30 m (100 ft.) to the left of the trail near a small clearing. The rock offers a dramatic view to the northwest. To the left, you can see Peters Mountain on the other side of Stony Creek valley, as well as several other distant ridges. The clearing is a popular campsite.

A little farther along the trail is the site of the old Stony Creek Fire Tower. The tower has been dismantled and removed, and all that remains are five concrete support blocks.

The trail now threads its way through a clearing, which gives a limited view to the east.

At 2.4 km (1.5 mi.) you will arrive at a double-blazed white oak that marks a trail junction. The Potts Mountain Trail begins here and runs straight ahead along the ridge. The AT turns right (south), skirting the eastern continental divide. The woods along the trail are pleasant.

At 3.5 km (2.2 mi.) you will pass close to Lone Pine Peak. The trail now starts a 610 m (2,000 ft.) descent to the floor of John's Creek valley.

You will arrive at the junction with the War Spur Connector to the Chestnut Trail at 4.2 km (2.6 mi.), after descending for 120 m (400 ft.). The AT turns left (east) here.

The AT continues to drop steeply for another 2.3 km (1.4 mi.). Now and then you may obtain some scenic glimpses of the valley ahead. The forest changes subtly as you descend.

War Spur Shelter appears suddenly on the left as you reach the foot of Salt Pond Mountain. There is water close-by.

Many mushrooms grow in this area in August. Don't eat any unless you know your mushrooms perfectly!

In another 0.8 km (0.5 mi.) you will reach County Road 632 in John's Creek valley near the spot where the road crosses John's Creek.

POTTS MOUNTAIN TRAIL

Length: 8 kilometers (5 miles)
Direction of travel: Generally northeast
Difficulty: Moderate to strenuous
Elevation: 1,240–897 meters (4,065–2,942 feet)
Difference in elevation: 343 meters (1,123 feet)
Markings: None
Trail # 55
How to get there: Via the Appalachian Trail. Follow it for 2.4 km (1.5 mi.) along the ridge of Potts Mountain to the junction marked by the double-blazed white oak. At this spot the AT turns right; the Potts Mountain Trail begins here and runs straight ahead.

If you wish to hike the trail in the opposite direction, drive west from Blacksburg on U.S. 460. At Newport turn right on Virginia Route 42. After roughly 19 km (12 mi.), watch for the spot where County Road 658 turns off to the left. Follow 658 to the village of Maggie. Then pick up County Road 636 where it leaves 658 (they run together for a short while) and drive as far as the Virginia-West Virginia state line. The Potts Mountain Trail (a jeep trail there) can be found on the left side of the road.

Trail description: At 1.6 km (1 mi.) from its beginning at the AT, the Potts Mountain Trail arrives at White Rocks in a high saddle of Potts Mountain, near the spot where Virginia's Giles and Craig counties meet West Virginia's Monroe County. The White Rocks are leaning slabs of bedrock, with a pretty view of John's Creek valley to the south. There are a few possible semi-sheltered campsites under the rocks, and there is a spring, at least in April, about 400 m down the John's Creek side of the mountain. It might be well, though, not to rely on the spring during drier months, when water usually is scarce along these ridges.

A few hundred meters past White Rocks there is an indistinct fork in the trail. The right-hand fork, the clearer of the two, is the White Rocks Trail, which leads down to John's Creek valley and County Road 632. The indistinct left fork is the continuation of the Potts Mountain Trail. Take the left fork.

The trail now winds around the peak of the ridge and then descends into West Virginia along an old, somewhat overgrown logging road. You will reach a clearing in 0.8 km (0.5 mi.).

A few hundred meters past the top of Eilber Springs Hollow, the Potts Mountain Trail peters out. The continuation of the trail as shown on the USGS map is nonexistent and, unless you are an addicted bushwacker, you will have to turn back here (8 km; 5 mi.).

Other, hardier souls who, in adddition to their determination, have a map and compass along, can attempt to follow the somewhat rocky ridgeline of Potts Mountain. Walk east and southeast from an unnamed 1,159 m (3,8000 ft. peak for a short distance, and then bend northeast to stay on the crest of the ridge.

After descending the ridge crest for 3.2 km (2 mi.), the bushwhacker will reach a rough jeep trail. Following it for 0.5 km (0.3 mi.) will lead to a long narrow clearing that marks the easternmost point of the Mountain Lake Wilderness.

The jeep trail runs through the clearing, which is posted against trespassing, until it meets County Road 636. (This road connects Maggie, Virginia, with Waiteville, West Virginia.)

WHITE ROCKS TRAIL

Length: 6 kilometers (3.7 miles)
Direction of travel: Generally southeast
Difficulty: Moderate
Elevation: 1,190–610 meters (3,900–2,000 feet)
Difference in elevation: 580 meters (1,900 feet)
Markings: None
How to get there: Via the Appalachian and Potts Mountain trails. The White Rocks Trail begins with the right-hand branch of an indistinct fork in the Potts Mountain Trail, a few hundred meters past White Rocks.

To hike the trail in the opposite direction, drive west from Blacksburg on U.S. 460. At Newport turn right on Virginia Route 42. After roughly 19 km (12 mi.), watch for the spot where County Road 658 turns off to the left. Follow 658 for 6.4 km (4 mi.) and turn left onto County Road 632 (before reaching the village of Maggie). The White Rocks Trail can be found on the right-hand side of the road, 5.5 km (3.4 mi.) after this final turn and 0.8 km (0.5 mi.) after a small pond on the right.
Trail description: Leaving the Potts Mountain Trail, the White Rocks Trail climbs over a gentle crest and then starts a

gradual descent toward John's Creek valley. The descent steepens as the trail winds through the woods.

After traveling 3.1 km (1.9 mi.), the trail meets an old logging road. The right turn leads to a private tract of land, which is posted against trespassing. Take the left turn to follow the trail, which now descends close to a ridge.

About 0.8 km (0.5 mi.) later, a jeep trail converges with the trail from the left. The jeep trail leads to an overgrown timber cut in Eliber Springs Hollow.

For 0.5 km (0.3 mi.) the boundary of the Mountain Lake Wilderness coincides with the White Rocks Trail before bending sharply to the southwest. From here on the trail is outside the wilderness area.

At this point a small stream angles in from the right and flows beside the road. There is evidence of timber cutting on the left.

In another 0.5 km (0.3 mi.) a second stream, Bee Branch, joins the first from the right. This confluence is not obvious because of a thick growth of rhododendrons.

At 0.6 km (0.4 mi.) past the confluence, the road crosses the stream and, a little later, turns left and crosses another stream, this time John's Creek.

From here the White Rocks Trail skirts the edge of a field until it ends at County Road 632. The small community of Maggie is about 7.2 km (4.5 mi.) to the left, and Captain—smaller still—is about 1.1 km (0.7 mi.) to the right.

JOHN'S CREEK TRAIL

Length: 4.8 kilometers (3 miles)
Direction of travel: Southwest
Difficulty: Moderate
Elevation: 641–915 meters (2,100–3,000 feet)
Difference in elevation: 274 meters (900 feet)
Markings: None

How to get there: Take U.S. 460 west from Blacksburg and turn north on Virginia Route 42 at Newport. After 0.8 km (0.5 mi.) turn left on County Road 601. Follow 601 through Clover Hollow to the small community of Captain. There, turn left onto County Road 632. Park your car before you reach the boundary of the Mountain Lake Wilderness, 2.4 km (1.5 mi.) from Captain.

You will have to retrace your steps on this trail, as there is no connecting trail to use for a circuit hike.

Trail description: The John's Creek Trail is a pleasant hike along the stream valley. The cleared land ends just about where the trail enters the wilderness area, and the rest of the walk is largely through woods, with some understory of mountain laurel and rhododendron. Some of the best hunting and fishing in the region is found in this valley.

As you walk along, the trail climbs a little, but it never becomes very steep. You will pass serveral tributaries, but crossing them should present no problem.

The trail ends high in John's Creek valley at a power line and right-of-way (4.8 km; 3 mi.).

If you wish to follow John's Creek to its source, you will have to bushwhack. You can follow the sound of the brook—except perhaps in late summer and fall—and, among the rhododendron and mountain laurel, you may find intermittent overgrown paths and logging trails. At 2.4 km (1.5 mi.) from the power line, you will reach the top of John's Creek drainage.

Another bushwhacking variation would be to follow the power line uphill. The going might be tough, though—a fair amount of brush probably grows along its entire length, and the right-of-way is steep. It passes within 30 m (100 ft.) of the summit of Bald Knob. This bushwhack is recommended only for the experienced and hardy.

GEORGE'S CUT HOLLOW AND HARVEY HOLLOW TRAILS

Length: 3.2 kilometers (2 miles)
Direction of travel: Generally south
Difficluty: Moderate
Elevation: 732–1,098 meters (2,400–3,600 feet)
Difference in elevation: 366 meters (1,200 feet)
Markings: None, trails difficult to reach and follow
How to get there: From Blacksburg, take U.S. 460 west, past Newport, and turn right on County Road 700. Follow 700, which is later numbered 613, past the Mountain Lake Hotel and the Mountain Lake Biological Station, and over Potts Mountain. In the valley on the other side, turn right on County Road 635 and drive 5.6 km (3.5 mi.) until you see the Jefferson National Forest boundary sign. Start your hike on the right near the sign, about 4 km (2.5 mi.) southwest of Waiteville, West Virginia.
Trail description: The beginning of this hike requires some imagination, a topographic map, and a good sense of direction.

From the point where you left your car, wind your way southward through a rambling rhododendron thicket, gaining elevation, until you arrive at an old railroad grade. This grade forms much of the northern boundary of the Mountain Lake Wilderness.

Here you will have to do some good guesswork: Walk along the grade, left or right, depending on where you met the grade, until you come to either George's Cut Hollow Trail or Harvey Hollow Trail.

George's Cut Hollow Trail is the easier trail to follow. It runs next to a cascading stream, with lots of rhododendrons growing along it. The trail is steep, but not unpleasantly so.

145

In 0.8 km (0.5 mi.) you will meet the Harvey Hollow Trail running in from the left.

Ascending instead via the Harvey Hollow Trail is a bit more difficult, as the path is rather obscure, and steeper. At the top of its ravine, Harvey Hollow Trail veers from its southward course to the west, skirting around the south side of a knob, until it joins George's Cut Hollow Trail.

Continue south along the trail from the junction. Little Mountain will be on the right, on the other side of a marshy stream. Soon you will ascend a gradual slope in a southeasterly direction.

About 0.5 km (0.3 mi.) later, the trail skirts a ridge and assumes a southwesterly direction while becoming nearly level.

In another 0.8 km (0.5 mi.) the terrain steepens and the trail peters out. The connecting section of trail to the Potts Mountain Trail shown on the USGS map does not exist. It is possible to bushwhack to the Potts Mountain Trail, but the going is difficult and only for the experienced. Everyone else should retrace his or her steps to County Road 635.

8. Peters Mountain Wilderness

The Peters Mountain Wilderness is a long, rather narrow corridor of 20.2 square kilometers (5,000 acres) on the southeastern flank of Peters Mountain, bordering Monroe County, West Virginia.

Biologically, Peters Mountain is closely related to the Mountain Lake Wilderness, containing much of the same vegetation. The Canadian Zone is represented by hemlocks near the top of Pine Swamp Branch and in some of the other drainages. Additional trees on Peters Mountain include chestnut oak, pitch pine, and upland oaks, mixed with stands of Virginia pine. Throughout the region there are table-mountain pine, yellow poplar, hickory, and red and white oaks. Rhododendrons form dense stands in well-watered places, and mountain laurel is plentiful on the higher dry ridges and slopes.

Trout abound in Stony Creek, which, along with County Road 635, forms the southeastern boundary of the wilderness. The rocks are mostly sedimentary, but we did not find any good places to look for fossils.

Average July temperatures in nearby Blacksburg and in Union, West Virginia, are in the low twenties Celsius (seventies, Fahrenheit), but individual days vary greatly. The average January temperatures in these two towns are around freezing, but a record low of minus 37 degrees Celsius (minus 34 degrees Fahrenheit) has been recorded in Union. So if you are planning a winter camping trip to Peters Mountain, go prepared for very cold weather! And, in any season, take rain gear, for showers are frequent.

In this area we have described the Appalachian Trail in two separate sections—one going southwest and the other northeast from the same spot. The reason for this division

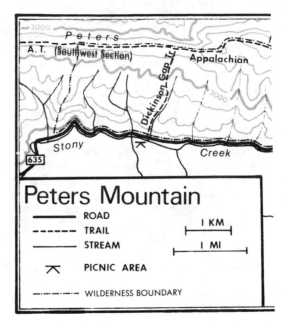

Mountain

Allegheny Trail

Dixon Branch Tr.

Trail

Shelter

Dismal Branch Tr.

North Fork Tr.

Kelly Flats Tr.

A.T.

(Northeast Section)

Picnic Area

N

635

is that the second section makes an easy afternoon walk, especially for families with small children. It is 2.6 kilometers (1.6 miles) long. Only half of that lies within the Peters Mountain Wilderness, but the entire hike is interesting—pretty woods, picturesque streams and hollows, and remains of old mines to explore. If you wish to hike the entire length of the AT within the area, merely join the two sections together. (You will have to read one trail description backward.)

Four trails—Kelly Flats, North Fork, Dixon Branch, and Dismal Branch—are also called the Flat Peter Loop. Unfortunately, some trails are not very well maintained and you may encounter difficulties in completing the loop.

The Virginia Tech Outing Club has put together descriptions and maps for additional trails not covered here. For information write to Trail Guides, Virginia Tech Outing Club, Box 538, Blacksburg, VA 24060.

No camping or fire permits are presently needed.

Maps: USGS Interior and Lindside quadrangles, 7.5 minute series.

DICKINSON GAP TRAIL

Length: 2.1 kilometers (1.3 miles)
Direction of travel: North
Difficulty: Moderate
Elevation: 640–1,007 meters (2,098–3,300 feet)
Difference in elevation: 367 meters (1,202 feet)
Markings: Blue blazes
How to get there: Go west on U.S. 460 from Blacksburg, through Newport and Pembroke. Before you get to the first bridge over the New River, turn north on County Road 635. A dirt road with a gate leads off to the left 12.1 km (7.5 mi.) from U.S. 460 (4.5 km or 2.8 mi. past the APG Lime Corporation plant). This is the trailhead for the Dickinson

Gap Trail. A double blue blaze is located directly across the road from the trailhead.

You can reach the other end of the trail via the Appalachian Trail (southwest section).

Trail description: A gate blocks vehicular access to the trail, which at this point is an old logging road.

The trail is fairly steep, ascending approximately 1 m in every 6. In places it is somewhat overgrown, but you should have no difficulties following it. It turns several times as it passes through the young-to-maturing forest. Occasional small clearings and brush piles along the way should provide glimpses of wildlife.

At 2.1 km (1.3 mi.) the trail reaches its junction with the Appalachian Trail on top of the Peters Mountain ridge in Dickinson Gap.

APPALACHIAN TRAIL (southwest section)

Length: 22.5 kilometers (14 miles)
Direction of travel: Northwest and southwest
Difficulty: Strenuous
Elevation: 719–1,206 meters (2,359–3,956 feet)
Difference in elevation: 487 meters (1,597 feet)
Markings: White blazes
Trail # 1
How to get there: Go west from Blacksburg on U.S. 460, through Newport and Pembroke. Before you get to the first bridge over the New River, turn north on County Road 635. About 8.8 km (5.5 mi.) past the APG Lime plant (about 16.1 km or 10 mi. from U.S. 460), you will pass a small store. From there drive 0.3 km (0.2 mi.) farther and park at one of the widened road sections. A Forest Service sign marks the wilderness area. The Appalachian Trail comes within 20 m of the road, and you can join it via a dirt road on the left just before County Road 635 crosses Stony Creek.

If you wish to hike the trail in the opposite direction, follow U.S. 460 west past the second bridge over the New River. Turn right onto County Road 641 1.1 km (0.7 mi.) beyond the bridge and just before a Subaru dealership. The trailhead for the AT is 0.4 km (0.2 mi.) from U.S. 460. Park on the roadside near the dealership. If you reach a fork on 641, you have missed the trailhead.

Trail description: Enter the woods to join the AT, with its white blazes, and turn left (uphill). After a short, steep stretch, the trail slopes gently. In 0.8 km (0.5 mi.) you will arrive at the Pine Swamp Branch Shelter. A nice stream flows nearby.

The trail soon steepens and passes rhododendrons and several stately hemlocks interspersed with unusual patches of moss-covered stones.

The trail reaches its steepest and rockiest place 0.8 km (0.5 mi.) from the shelter, but starts to level off quickly. A little farther on, it enters the pine swamp for which Pine Swamp Branch was named.

After passing the swamp, you will gain the long ridge of Peters Mountain, which extends all the way to the New River. The Allegheny Trail joins the Appalachian Trail from the right at the crest. (We have not covered the Allegheny Trail because most of it lies outside the area described here.) The Appalachian Trail stays on the ridge for 13.8 km (8.6 mi.), providing occasional glimpses into West Virginia. The ridge is the dividing line between Virginia and West Virginia and marks the boundary of the Peters Mountain Wilderness.

The Dickinson Gap Trail joins the AT at 5.6 km (3.5 mi.) on the left. Down it, it is 2.1 km (1.3 mi.) to County Road 635.

The AT crosses the southern boundary of the wilderness area 2.1 km (1.3 mi.) past the junction with the Dickinson Gap Trail.

At Symm's Gap, 3.7 km (2.3 mi.) after the Dickinson Gap Trail, an old woods road crosses the AT leading down the slopes into West Virginia (right) and Virginia (left). You will find a fine view of several ridges and valleys in West Virginia here. Then the trees close in around you, and the view is lost.

The trail continues, with gentle ups and downs, along the ridge of Peters Mountain. It crosses a power line at 16.1 km (10 mi.). Finally it descends the mountainside steeply before reaching U.S. 460 and the New River at 22.5 km (14 mi.).

APPALACHIAN TRAIL (northeast section)

Length: 2.6 kilometers (1.6 miles)
Direction of travel: Generally east
Difficulty: Easy
Elevation: 719–793 meters (2,359–2,600 feet)
Difference in elevation: 74 meters (241 feet)
Markings: White blazes
Trail # 1
How to get there: Drive west from Blacksburg on U.S. 460, through Newport and Pembroke. Before reaching the first bridge over the New River, turn north on County Road 635. About 8.8 km (5.5 mi.) past the APG Lime plant (about 16.1 km or 10 mi. from U.S. 460), you will pass a small store. From there drive 0.3 km (0.2 mi.) farther and park at one of the widened road sections. A Forest Service sign marks the wilderness area. The AT comes within 20 m of the road, and you can join it via a dirt road on the left just before 635 crosses Stony Creek.

To hike in the opposite direction, continue 2.5 km (1.5 mi.) beyond the bridge across Stony Creek. The AT crosses County Road 635 shortly after the Forest Service's Interior Picnic Area. A signpost marks the intersection. There is a small parking area close-by. A sturdy footbridge leads the AT over Stony Creek at this point.

Only the first half of this walk is in the Peters Mountain Wilderness; the second half runs through other national forest property.

Trail description: Follow the white blazes to the right (north), bypassing the left-hand uphill turnoff to the Pine Swamp Branch Shelter.

For a short distance, the trail stays close to the bank of Stony Creek, then crosses two small tributaries in quick succession. It briefly turns away from the stream and gains a little altitude, but quickly returns to its course.

Several trailers and a cinder block hunting lodge are situated on the far side of the creek in a large crescent-shaped clearing. Halfway around this bend, you will cross a third small tributary in a narrow ravine, with some hemlocks and rhododendrons. Two high, steep hollows converge 0.5 km (0.3 mi.) uphill to form this stream.

The AT now bends around the base of a large hill and runs onto an old railroad of mining-car grade. It follows the grade and turns left with it in front of a stream, where there are a series of picturesque step falls.

There is an old rock foundation on the stream bank near the falls. It may have formed the base for a mill years ago. Or perhaps it was associated with the abandoned mining operations that left a series of graded mounds and slopes for a distance of about 0.8 km (0.5 mi.) upstream. The mounds and slopes must be fairly old, as several good-sized trees are growing around them.

The AT now turns right and crosses the stream on a small log and plank footbridge. A short grassy spot is followed by another somewhat larger stream, with another, larger log and plank bridge. This is the Dismal Branch.

Just past this crossing, the AT joins a woods road, which forms part of the boundary of the Peters Mountain Wilderness. Left (upstream), the woods road is the Kelly Flats Trail and leads to the beginning of the Dismal Branch Trail. The AT follows this road to the right for 0.2 km (0.1 mi.), then angles uphill to the left.

The AT continues to the left up the crest of a narrow ridge, which it follows for a short way through some rhododendrons. It then cuts downhill on the right side of the ridge toward Stony Creek. The descent leads through a pleasant, mature mixed forest, with hemlocks here and there, and lots of rhododendrons lower on the slope.

After reaching the floodplain of Stony Creek, the AT completes the final short stretch under a cool canopy of pines, hemlocks, and occasional holly trees.

At 2.6 km (1.6 mi.) the trail crosses Stony Creek on a large, new wooden footbridge to arrive at County Road 635 and the small parking lot.

DISMAL BRANCH TRAIL

Length: 3.3 kilometers (2.1 miles)
Direction of travel: North
Difficulty: Moderate
Elevation: 765–1,040 meters (2,510–3,400 feet)
Difference in elevation: 275 meters (890 feet)
Markings: Yellow blazes
How to get there: Via the Appalachian Trail (northeast section) and the Kelly Flats Trail. The Dismal Branch Trail starts off the Kelly Flats Trail, which is an old woods road, about 0.5 km (0.3 mi.) after it branches off the AT.
Trail description: Walk along Kelly Flats Trail for 0.5 km (0.3 mi.), crossing two streams. Turn left onto Dismal Branch Trail, which appears as a wide road at this point.

Later the road becomes a true foot trail, narrow and rougher. The trail climbs steeply up the Dismal Branch drainage, meandering back and forth across the stream, and sometimes following in its bed, through dark, cool rhododendron thickets.

The head of the Dismal Branch watershed, the wildest and quietest part of Peters Mountain, is a high, isolated, and shallow valley protected by Pine Swamp Ridge on the south, Huckleberry Ridge on the east, and the crest of Peters Mountain on the northwest.

Depending upon how recently a trail maintenance crew has been through, you may or may not have difficulty in locating the junction with the Dixon Branch Trail on the right.

There are tentative plans to extend Dismal Branch Trail to connect with the Allegheny Trail on the crest of Peters Mountain. Until this extension is actually built, you will have to bushwhack to reach the top.

KELLY FLATS TRAIL

Length: 3.3 kilometers (2.0 miles)
Direction of travel: East
Difficulty: Easy
Elevation: 744–779 meters (2,440–2,555 feet)
Difference in elevation: 35 meters (115 feet)
Markings: Yellow blazes
How to get there: Take U.S. 460 west through Newport and Pembroke. Go north on County Road 635 for 21.7 km (13.5 mi.) until you come to a gravel road. Turn left here and cross a small bridge. Park your car, but be careful not to block a gate on the right leading to private property.

The other end can be reached via the Appalachian Trail (northeast section).

Trail description: The Kelly Flats Trail starts with the *left* branch of the road, which also has a gate.

The Kelly Flats Trail follows the road for 1.1 km (0.7 mi.), then enters a long clearing about 40 m wide. Toward the end of the clearing, at 1.7 km (1.1 mi.), Dismal Branch Trail leads off to the right.

Another 0.5 km (0.3 mi.) will bring you to the AT. A left turn will take you to the Interior Picnic Area at County Road 635. Turn right and you will eventually ascend toward the Pine Swamp Branch shelter.

The Kelly Flats Trail is not a particularly interesting trail—it has been flattened, in parts plowed over and cleared for game. It does, however, provide access to trails that lead to some more beautiful areas uphill.

NORTH FORK TRAIL

Length: 5.6 kilometers (3.5 miles)
Direction of travel: North
Difficulty: Moderate
Elevation: 779–896 meters (2,555–2,940 feet)
Difference in elevation: 117 meters (385 feet)
Markings: Yellow blazes
How to get there: Take U.S. 460 west through Newport and Pembroke. Go north on County Road 635 for 21.7 km (13.5 mi.) until you come to a gravel road. Turn left here and cross a small bridge. Park your car, but be careful not to block a gate on the right leading to private property.
Trail description: Follow the *center* branch of the gated road for 0.6 km (0.4 mi.). The North Fork Trail turns right into the woods here.

At first you will have to watch carefully for the trail. The blazes are intermittent, sometimes as far as 100 m apart.

At 1.7 km (1.1 mi.) the trail crosses the creek, then follows an old railroad grade. The forest scenery is much more interesting and pleasant than that of the Kelly Flats Trail.

Once it enters the North Fork ravine, the trail becomes easy to follow to its junction at 5.6 km (3.5 mi.) with a woods road to the right and the Dixon Branch Trail to the left.

DIXON BRANCH TRAIL

Length: 3.5 kilometers (2.2 miles)
Direction of travel: West
Difficulty: Difficult
Elevation: 896–1,036 meters (2,940–3,400 feet)
Difference in elevation: 140 meters (460 feet)
Markings: Yellow blazes
How to get there: The trail starts at the end of the North Fork Trail. Depending on how recently a trail maintenance crew has been through, the other end may be reached via the Dismal Branch Trail.
Trail description: The Dixon Branch Trail follows a northerly course for 200 m after the woods road veers off to the right at the junction with the North Fork Trail. Then Dixon Branch Trail turns sharply to the left (west) and begins to climb along the north side of Huckleberry Ridge, crossing a creek several times.

It enters a beautiful wild area, with rhododendrons growing thickly along the way. Unfortunately, the rhododendrons make the trail hard to follow and, depending on how recently the last trail maintenance crew has come through, at some points it is impenetrable.

Should you find your way thus barred, retrace your steps. Hardy souls can attempt to bushwhack up the right-hand side of the ravine to the top of Peters Mountain and the Allegheny Trail along its ridge. A left turn on the Allegheny

Trail will take you to its junction with the Appalachian Trail near the top of Pine Swamp Branch.

The Dixon Branch Trail continues its sometimes steep ascent through the rhododendron thickets to Huckleberry Ridge and thence descends to the junction with Dismal Branch Trail.

9. Mill Creek Area

The Mill Creek Area, in Jefferson National Forest, is a shallow valley on a high mountain bounded by steep, almost impassable cliffs. The cliffs make the valley very picturesque, and the mountain crests offer outstanding views of the surrounding countryside. Narrows and Pearisburg are the nearest towns.

A large part of the area was logged and burned before the U.S. Forest Service acquired the land in the early part of the century. Some mining activities, particularly for manganese, also were carried on for a while. Since Forest Service acquisition, however, the land has been managed as a watershed for the town of Narrows, and logging has ceased. Hunting, hiking, and fishing are now the main activities. The old logging roads have been reseeded as wildlife trails, but can still be followed fairly easily. If you feel adventurous enough to try such exploration, do carry a compass and topographic map to orient yourself. The only incursions by civilization are two power lines that cross the area near its center.

The forest cover contains typical Appalachian hardwoods predominantly oaks as well as pitch pine and Virginia pine. Occasionally you will encounter table-mountain pine, yellow poplar, red and white oaks, and hickory. Rhododendrons and azaleas grow in abundance. Both Mercy Branch and Mill Creek, the two main streams in the valley, support native trout.

Temperatures are cooler than in cities and lowlands. Winds on exposed rocks can be chilly in summer and biting in winter. Be sure to take adequate clothing! Rain gear against a sudden shower or thunderstorm should be included.

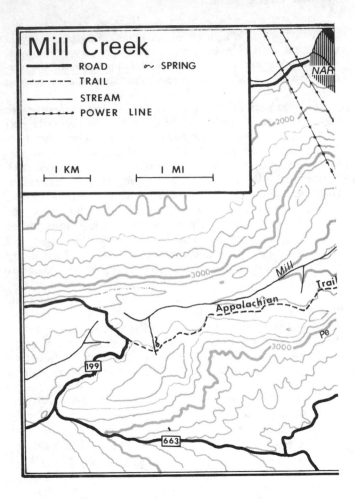

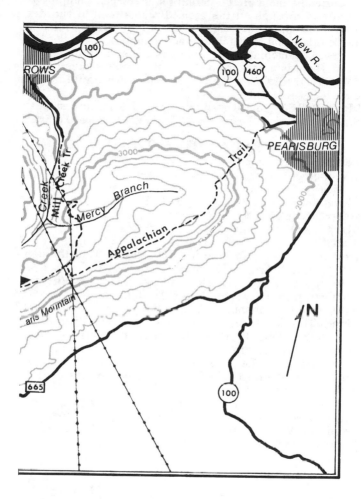

Currently, there are no permit requirements. Camping is permitted throughout the area. Streams tend to run dry toward the end of the year, and water may not be available on the ridges and mountaintops at any time.

The Appalachian Trail traverses the area from east to west. There is a shelter on it near the area's southernmost point. The Mill Creek Trail is the only other useful hiking trail.

Maps: USGS Narrows quadrangle, 7.5 minute series; Blacksburg Ranger District map, Jefferson National Forest.

APPALACHIAN TRAIL

Length: 12.9 kilometers (8 miles)
Direction of travel: Generally southwest
Difficulty: Strenuous
Elevation: 610–1,150 meters (2,000–3,770 feet)
Difference in elevation: 540 meters (1,770 feet)
Markings: White blazes
Trail # 1
How to get there: To hike the Appalachian Trail through the Mill Creek Area, you will need a car shuttle.

To reach the northern end of the trail, take the Virginia Tech exit from Interstate 81 to U.S. 460. Follow U.S. 460 to the second Pearisburg exit (BUSINESS 460 EAST HIGHWAY 100 SOUTH). Turn left (south) onto Johnston Avenue and drive about 150 m (500 ft.), then turn right onto Morris Avenue. Continue for 1.3 km (0.8 mi.). until the road makes a sharp right turn. The AT leaves Morris Avenue on the left-hand side of the road, where the road has been widened to accomodate parking for a few cars.

To reach the southern end of the trail, drive west from Blacksburg on U.S. 460 into Pearisburg and turn left (south) on Virginia Route 100. Drive 3.2 km (2 mi) to the junction with County Rd 665. Turn right onto 665 and drive to its end at County Road 663 (7.2 km; 4.5 mi.). Turn right onto 663 and continue past the end of state maintenance. The road becomes very poor and may not be passable to ordinary vehicles. If there is a gate on the road, open it for passage and be sure to close it behind you. Continue on the road to a fork, and turn right onto Route 199. The road is part of the AT there, and you will be able to see white blazes on the trees. Continue for 1.6 km (1 mi.) until the trail turns to the right at a parking place, where a sign marks the Mill Creek watershed.

Trail description: Leaving Morris Avenue, the AT first crosses a telephone right-of-way, then a dirt road twice. The second road crossing displaces the trail 100 m to the right. The trail ascends steeply for the first 2.1 km (1.3 mi.). The climb to View Rock, toward the end, is almost vertical. But View Rock is appropriately named and worth the effort. From the top you will have an outstanding view of the New River valley and the town of Pearisburg.

The AT then runs through rhododendrons and between large rock slabs. Before it reaches Angels Rest (1,083 m; 3,550 ft.), a blue-blazed spur trail leading to a spring 0.3 km (0.2 mi.) down the ridge joins the AT.

Following the edge of Pearis Mountain, the trail passes by a large rock ledge that overhangs the Wilburn Valley. The view of the New River valley to the east is spectacular. Geologists believe the New River is the oldest river channel in the Western Hemisphere. Long-time power company plans to build two dams on the New River at Galax and Independence, to the south, were thwarted when 42.6 km (26.5 mi.) of the waterway became part of the National Wild and Scenic Rivers System in September 1976.

The trail now runs, with minor ups and downs, along the ridge of Pearis Mountain. At 6.4 km (4 mi.) it passes under a power line; the Mill Creek Trail dead-ends here from the right. The AT then runs downhill sharply to the right.

In a short while you will come upon an old logging road. The path turns left here.

The Appalachian Trail passes under a second power line. Here is another viewpoint, this time to the right and toward the town of Narrows.

The next section of the trail is beautiful in the spring, with many flowering rhododendrons and azaleas.

At 12.1 km (7.5 mi.) you will arrive at a shelter and spring. Shortly thereafter, at 12.9 km (8 mi.), you will meet the fire road that marks the southwestern boundary of the area described here.

MILL CREEK TRAIL

Length: 3.4 kilometers (2.1 miles)
Direction of travel: South
Difficulty: Moderate to strenuous
Elevation: 580–941 meters (1,900–3,085 feet)
Difference in elevation: 361 meters (1,185 feet)
Markings: None; trail at times difficult to follow
How to get there: Drive west from Blacksburg on U.S. 460 past Pearisburg to the business district exit of Narrows. Take this exit into town to the junction with Highway 100. Turn left, go 0.5 km (0.3 mi.), then turn right onto Northview Street (County Road 652). Continue to the end of the road (2 km; 1.2 mi.) and park your car.

The other end of the trail can be reached via the Appalachian Trail.
Trail description: The trail starts as an old logging road at the end of Northview Street.

Climb over a small berm and pass through some weeds to reach the road that runs parallel to Mill Creek. This is actually a power line access road, but also the easiest way to reach the AT on top of the ridge.

The road curves sharply left at 0.5 km (0.3 mi.), away from Mill Creek. It reaches the power line 1 km (0.6 mi.) later.

The access road is fairly well maintained. It crosses back and forth under the power line several times before staying on the east side until it gets within 50 m of the AT. There are many beautiful views of the New River and the town of Narrows whenever the trail passes under the power lines.

Mill Creek Trail crosses under the power lines once more before joining the AT as it descends from the crest of Pearis Mountain.

To the right, it is 6.4 km (4 mi.) along the AT to Route 199; to the left, it is 6.4 km (4 mi.) to the town of Pearisburg.

10. Mount Rogers National Recreation Area

Mount Rogers National Recreation Area lies in southwestern Virginia near its border with Tennessee and North Carolina, immediately south of the town of Marion. Mount Rogers, at 1,747 meters (5,729 feet), Whitetop Mountain to the west (1,690 meters; 5,540 feet), and Pine Mountain to the east (1,685 meters; 5,526 feet) form a ridge of the highest mountains in the state. The northwestern part is the Lewis Fork Wilderness, to the east is Little Wilson Creek Wilderness, and Grayson Highlands State Park lies just to the south.

There are some private inholdings in the recreation area, especially to the south, but no trails cross private property. The one road that does—not described here—is used mainly by people whose livestock graze by lease on national forest land. Grazing, of course, keeps a meadow a meadow.

The area is unique in several aspects. Fraser fir and red spruce grow on the summits of Mount Rogers and Whitetop Mountain. These species usually are found farther south on the higher mountains of the southern Appalachians. At a lower elevation, you will find northern hardwoods such as eastern hemlock, yellow birch, beech, and northern red oak—trees that generally grow much farther north. Below these two distinct zones grow trees much more common to central and western Virginia, such as oak and hickory.

Pine Mountain is a high plateau of open meadows and scattered woods, which give the region an Alpine look. Rhododendrons, azaleas, and rock outcrops, as well as grazing sheep, add to that appearance. In the spring you will find many wildflowers in the woods and meadows.

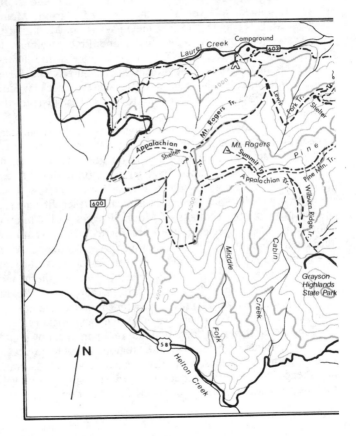

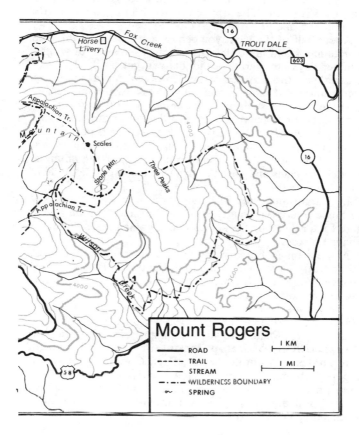

Horse
Livery

Fox Creek

16

TROUT DALE

603

Appalachian Tr.

M o u n t a i n

Scales

4000

16

Stone Mtn.

Three Peaks

Appalachian Tr.

Wilson

Creek

4000

4000

58

Mount Rogers

——— ROAD
- - - TRAIL
——— STREAM
-··-··- WILDERNESS BOUNDARY
∼ SPRING

|——| 1 KM

|——| 1 MI

The streams support some fish. Deer and various other animals, as well as a large number of birds, can be observed readily.

If you plan to hike in the recreation area, get a good road map of Virginia. The approach to the region is quite complicated, and you will need the map badly.

About half of the year, you can expect frost at night. The mountaintops and high plateaus are snow-covered in winter. Summer days are warm, but nights can get chilly. It is not unusual at the higher elevations to have freezing temperatures and snow in mid-May, so take warm clothes.

There are two shelters in the area: Old Orchard on the north slope of Pine Mountain and the other at Deep Gap. Both are heavily used. Livestock graze in much of the region, especially around Pine Mountain, and the fences you will find across trails are there to confine grazing animals. Unlatch the gates and pass through, but be sure to latch them shut after you.

If you are interested in horses, you may want to stop at the horse livery on County Road 603. Horses can be rented there for a ride along the specially designated trails that have orange markers.

A great many horse trails have sprung up in the area. Other trails have been abandoned and receive no maintenance. You can still find some of these paths. Avoid getting lost by carrying a compass and a map.

Many trails have springs running across them and are wet and boggy—often because they have been used by wild ponies as well. Make sure you wear appropriate footgear.

Maps: USGS Whitetop Mountain and Trout Dale quadrangles, 7.5 minute series; High Country Trails, Mt. Rogers National Recreation Area, compiled and edited by Larry Landrum, cartography by Susan Woodward, ©1985 by Larry Landrum (write Larry Landrum, P.O. Box 247, Blacksburg, VA 24060).

MOUNT ROGERS TRAIL

Length: 7.2 kilometers (4.5 miles)
Direction of travel: South
Difficulty: Moderate
Elevation: 1,098–1,495 meters (3,600–4,900 feet)
Difference in elevation: 397 meters (1,300 feet)
Markings: Light blue blazes
Trail # 166

How to get there: Use your Virginia road map to get to Trout Dale. Then take County Road 603 west for 10.2 km (6.3 mi.) to a small parking area on the side of the road. The trail starts there, on the left (south) side of the road. You can also join the trail via a spur leaving from Grindstone Campground 0.3 km (0.2 mi.) farther along 603.

You can reach the other end of the trail via the Appalachian Trail.

Trail description: Starting on a wooden walkway, the Mount Rogers Trail climbs steadily to its junction with the Grindstone Campground spur at 0.3 km (0.2 mi.).

There are a couple of switchbacks not too far from the campground. After that the trail ascends fairly straight up along the hillside. The first half of the trail is smooth, with few rocks. It climbs through a diverse deciduous forest, comprising magnolia, oak, birch, and beech.

A creek runs for the most part close to the trail, in a little valley of its own. At 3.3 km (2 mi.) the Lewis Fork Trail (dark blue blazes) branches off to the left. After this junction the trail becomes more primitive—rockier and at times also wetter. The forest changes from all hardwoods to a mixture with evergreens. The ferns and mosses under the trees suggest much moisture in the air.

The Mount Rogers Trail traverses the Lewis Fork Wilderness, as does indeed the Lewis Fork Trail, for almost its entire length.

The trail continues to climb on a moderate grade along the side of Mount Rogers until it meets the Appalachian Trail about 7.2 km (4.5 mi.) from the campground. To the right on the AT it is 3.1 km (1.9 mi.) to County Road 600. The Deep Gap Shelter is approximately 0.2 km (0.1 mi.) to the right on the AT. A blue-blazed side trail near it leads to a spring.

APPALACHIAN TRAIL

Length: 27.2 kilometers (16.9 miles)
Direction of travel: East and north
Difficulty: Strenuous
Elevation: 1,357–1,647–1,067 meters (4,450–5,400–3,500 feet)
Difference in elevation: 290–579 meters (950–1,900 feet)
Markings: White blazes
Trail # 1
How to get there: Use your Virginia road map to get to Trout Dale. Then follow County Road 603 west for 17.4 km (10.8 mi.) to County Road 600. Turn left (south) on 600 and drive about 8 km (5 mi.) to the grassy saddle between Whitetop Mountain and Mount Rogers. The AT starts on the east side of the road.

For a hike in the opposite direction, go west from Trout Dale on County Road 603 for 4.8 km (3 mi.) to the horse livery. The AT starts about 1.5 km (0.9 mi.) past it, on the left.

Trail description: After passing through the gate at the trailhead on County Road 600, you have the choice of following the marked trail (white blazes) to the left or the obvious woods road, which is also a horse trail (orange blazes), to the right. If you opt for the latter, remember that horses have the right of way. And watch your step!

Hiking along the Appalachian Trail, watch carefully for the blazes; they are sometimes hard to see. There is no water along this stretch. At first the AT passes through a meadow, ascending to a knob with a good view. Continue across the meadow and cross a stile. The trail generally follows the ridge of Elk Garden Mountain, though skirting the top. At 3.1 km (1.9 mi.) the AT passes Deep Gap Shelter. A spring can be found approximately 200 m away via a blue-blazed side trail. The horse trail also passes the shelter.

After an additional 0.2 km (0.1 km) the AT meets the Mount Rogers Trail, coming up from Grindstone Campground and County Road 603.

The Appalachian Trail now ascends a rocky, brambly slope and then enters a spruce forest. After a couple of switchbacks—sometimes climbing steeply—the trail levels off. About 1.2 km (0.7 mi.) after the junction with the Mount Rogers Trail the AT makes a sharp left turn. Watch the blazes. It does not cross the fence or go into the meadow beyond. There are some fine views over the fence and across the meadow.

Continue along the AT through the woods. Here the trees are older and the forest is therefore more open. Several small streams run through the area.

At 6.1 km (3.8 mi.) the trail to the summit of Mount Rogers branches off to the left.

The AT now passes through open meadows with scattered firs, providing truly scenic hiking.

At 8 km (5 mi.), at Rhododendron Gap, a somewhat confusing intersection occurs. Follow the blazes carefully. The AT makes a sharp right turn, while the Pine Mountain Trail—blazed pale blue—continues straight ahead. The Wilburn Ridge Trail, also with blue blazes, runs generally parallel to the AT, crossing over the rock outcrops. You will pass rhododendron thickets—this spot is called Rhododendron Gap—shortly after the trail junction. The flowering bushes look very pretty in early June.

From Rhododendron Gap the AT skirts to the right of Wilburn Ridge and follows a more gentle descent toward Massie Gap in Grayson Highlands State Park. Two springs can be found along this section of the trail.

After 2.4 km (1.5 mi.) cross a fence—the Wilburn Ridge Trail rejoins the AT shortly before this point—which is the boundary between national forest land and the state park. Shortly thereafter you will come to a trail, blazed blue, leading to Massie Gap in 0.8 km (0.5 mi.).

Here the AT bears sharply left. Follow the white blazes carefully at all times. The trail ascends gradually, crossing and recrossing the boundary between national forest and state park. Wilson Creek even sports a wooden bridge. A horse trail intersects shortly hereafter, leading, to the right, eventually to the state park campground.

The AT now skirts a peak, and for a brief stretch you will find yourself in the Little Wilson Creek Wilderness. Then the AT turns north again, crosses another horse trail, and passes out of the wilderness.

If you follow the horse trail to the right you can visit the Three Peaks—some with good views—and eventually loop back to the AT at Scales.

Continuing along the AT, climb toward the crest of Stone Mountain. There are nice views along this stretch. Descend slightly to Scales, where you will find a small fenced-in area used as a corral for the cattle that graze this area in the summer.

At 21.1 km (13.1 mi.) you will come to the junction with the Pine Mountain Trail, leading back to Rhododendron Gap. Turn right to follow the AT's white blazes.

The trail now descends steadily, winding back and forth. It is fairly rocky in places, and the grade is sometimes steep. The forest changes from evergreen to deciduous woodlands.

At 24.3 km (15.1 mi.) you will arrive at the Old Orchard Shelter. There is a spring close-by. The shelter overlooks a meadow. Mount Rogers can be glimpsed to the left.

Just below the shelter the AT crosses a wide trail blazed blue. This is the Old Orchard Trail, which leads to the Lewis Fork Trail.

Follow the AT downhill through deciduous woods to meet County Road 603 at 27.2 km (16.9 mi.).

SUMMIT TRAIL

Length: 0.8 kilometers (0.5 mile)
Direction of travel: Northwest
Difficulty: Moderate to easy
Elevation: 1,647–1,747 meters (5,400–5,729 feet)
Difference in elevation: 100 meters (329 feet)
Markings: Blue blazes; trail easy to follow
Trail # 4590
How to get there: Via the Appalachian Trail, 6.1 km (3.8 mi.) from County Road 600 or 10.3 km (6.4 mi.) from County Road 603, near Grindstone Campground. The trailhead is located west of Rhododendron Gap, on Mount Rogers's eastern slope.
Trail description: At one time the Appalachian Trail crossed the top of Mount Rogers, but it has now been relocated and the summit is reached by a short side trail.

This access trail ascends gradually through a somewhat overgrown meadow. It then enters spruce and fir forest. The vegetation remains the same to the summit.

The peak of Mount Rogers is wooded and affords no views. There were quite a few dead and fallen trees on the northeast slopes of the mountain when we were there. A

177

marker is located at the highest point: 1,747 m (5,729 ft.). This is the highest mountain in Virginia.

You will have to retrace your steps to return to the AT and other trails.

WILBURN RIDGE TRAIL

Length: 2.3 kilometers (1.4 miles)
Direction of travel: Northwest
Difficulty: Easy
Elevation: 1,418–1,678 meters (4,650–5,500 feet)
Difference in elevation: 260 meters (850 feet)
Markings: Blue blazes
How to get there: Use your Virginia road map to get to Trout Dale. Then drive south on Virginia Route 16 to Volney. Turn right on U.S. 58 and drive 14.2 km (8.8 mi.) to the turnoff to Grayson Highlands State Park. Take the road into the park and follow it to the trailhead near a grassy area with picnic tables. Park on the shoulder of the road. The gate into the park is closed from 10 P.M. to 8 A.M., and camping is not permitted within the fenced-in area.

The other end of the trail can be reached via the Appalachian Trail.

Trail description: Leaving the road in Grayson Highlands State Park, proceed northward up the first part of Wilburn Ridge, reaching the Appalachian Trail after 0.8 km (0.5 mi.). Shortly after crossing the fence marking the boundary between national forest land and the state park, the Wilburn Ridge Trail branches off to the right.

After a short while you will top out on a rise. Then the trail climbs more gently.

The entire area of Wilburn Ridge and Pine Mountain is very open, and bushwhacking presents no problem. You can strike out across country at your whim. Do take a compass and a map if you are planning on a bushwhack.

Scattered woods provide a pleasant interruption from the open meadows. The view is excellent along almost the entire trail.

Continue hiking to the northwest. The Wilburn Ridge Trail crosses a number of rock outcrops. Scattered spruce are on your right. Mount Rogers and, in the distance, Whitetop Mountain are to your left.

At 2.3 km (1.4 mi.) the trail ends at the intersection with the Appalachian Trail and the Pine Mountain Trail. This junction is located in what is known as Rhododendron Gap. It is a beautiful area to visit early in June when the bushes are in full bloom.

PINE MOUNTAIN TRAIL

Length: 3.4 kilometers (2.1 miles)
Direction of travel: Northeast
Difficulty: Easy
Elevation: 1,524–1,646 meters (5,000–5,400 feet)
Difference in elevation: 122 meters (400 feet)
Markings: Pale blue blazes
Trail # 4595
How to get there: Via the Appalachian Trail.
Trail description: Coming from Massie Gap and Grayson Highlands State Park, follow the AT for 3.2 km (2 mi.) to Rhododendron Gap. Here take a right turn onto Pine Mountain Trail. Last time we were there no trail sign could be located, just the pale blue blazes. An orange-blazed horse trail runs parallel to the Pine Mountain Trail for much of the way.

Shortly after the junction, the Pine Mountain Trail descends into a rocky gully. For the first kilometer or so the trail threads its way through shoulder-high rhododendron—a spectacular sight in June when they bloom. Some taller rhododendrons and forest follow before the trail reaches open meadows again.

About halfway, at 1.6 km (1 mi.), the Cliff Trail, blazed in pink, branches off to the left and down the mountain to its junction with the Lewis Fork Trail and beyond. The only sign at this point tells you the distance to the Old Orchard Shelter via the Pine Mountain Trail (5.4 km; 3.3 mi.).

The Pine Mountain Trail continues through open meadows, with rhododendrons and occasional patches of hardwoods and evergreens, to its intersection with the AT at Pine Mountain. A sign there proclaims the elevation as 1,524 m (5,000 ft.).

From here it is about 3.2 km (2 mi.) to the Old Orchard Shelter via the AT.

LEWIS FORK TRAIL

Length: 5 kilometers (3 miles)
Direction of travel: Generally east to west
Difficulty: Moderate
Elevation: 1,220–1,414 meters (4,000–4,640 feet)
Difference in elevation: 195 meters (640 feet)
Markings: Dark blue blazes
Trail # 4533.3
How to get there: Via the Appalachian Trail and Old Orchard Trail or via the Mount Rogers Trail.
Trail description: Hiking up the Appalachian Trail from County Road 603, just before you reach the Old Orchard Shelter, you will come to a wide trail blazed in blue. Turn right here. Forest Service maps call this the Old Orchard Trail.

About 0.5 km (0.3 mi.) from the AT the trail forks. The right fork is the continuation of the Old Orchard Trail and returns to 603. The left fork, blazed dark blue, is the Lewis Fork Trail. Take the left fork (uphill).

This trail traverses the Lewis Fork Wilderness. It starts out as a fairly wide woods road and ascends gently but steadily. The entire length of the trail runs through woods, and there are no views along the way.

After about 1.6 km (1 mi.) you will cross a tributary creek to Lewis Fork. Just beyond it is the junction with the Cliff Trail (pink blazes). To the left the Cliff Trail ascends steeply toward the Pine Mountain Trail; to the right it continues its course downhill to an eventual junction with the Old Orchard Trail.

Continue following the dark blue blazes of the Lewis Fork Trail uphill. In another 1.6 km (1 mi.) you will come to Lewis Fork. Many rhododendrons grow along its banks. There is no bridge and you will have to hop across on rocks.

Shortly hereafter the trail forks. The left fork follows the creek to its source and dead-ends there at 0.8 km (0.5 mi.). You will have to retrace your steps to continue the hike.

You will reach another fork 0.2 km (0.1 mi.) farther. The old roadbed the trail followed up to now continues straight ahead, while the actual trail, with its blazes, jogs sharply to the left and begins a steep climb uphill. The turn is marked by a double blue blaze.

The Lewis Fork Trail continues climbing steeply, with few turns, until it meets the Mount Rogers Trail at 5 km (3 mi.). To the right is Grindstone Campground and County Road 603, to the left the junction with the Appalachian Trail.

Suggested Readings

Birds of North America: A Guide to Field Identification by Chandler S. Robbins, Bertel Bruun, and Herbert S. Zim; published by Golden Press, New York. A handy guide for field identification of birds both at home and on the trail.

Guide to the Appalachian Trail in Central and Southwestern Virginia; published by the Appalachian Trail Conference, Harpers Ferry, West Virginia. This book contains much useful information on camping and backpacking.

Trees of North America by C. Frank Brockman; published by Golden Press, New York. A guide to the identification of trees.

Walking Softly in the Wilderness, A Sierra Club Guide to Backpacking by John Hart; published by Sierra Club Books, San Francisco.

About the Author

Karin Wuertz-Schaefer is a member of the Sierra Club and worked for several years on the club's New York staff. She now lives in the Washington D.C. area where she works as a teacher of German, a translator, and a freelance writer.

Karin and her husband, Bob, a physicist, have been involved in local efforts to establish wilderness areas in Virginia. The idea for *Hiking Virginia's National Forests* grew from this involvement. With the help of friends involved in conservation movements, Karin has continued to update and expand the book, now in its fourth popular edition.